The Mystery and Magic Series

Magicians
and
Fairies

Robert Ingpen & Molly Perham

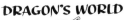

DRAGON'S WORLD

CHILDREN'S BOOKS

Dragon's World Ltd
Limpsfield
Surrey RH8 0DY
Great Britain

First published by Dragon's World Ltd, 1995

Editor: Diana Briscoe
Designer: Megra Mitchell
Design Assistants:
Karen Ferguson
Victoria Furbisher
Art Director: John Strange
Editorial Director: Pippa Rubinstein

British Library Cataloguing in Publication Data
The catalogue record for this book is available from the British Library.

ISBN 1 85028 301 X

Typeset by Dragon's World Ltd in Caslon, Century Old Style and Helvetica.
Printed in Italy

✳ Contents ✳

☀ Introduction ☀

In the pages of this book you can enter a fantasy world peopled with fairy spirits – nymphs and fauns, dwarves and goblins, leprechauns and pixies, magic cats and talking trees. You will meet peries and genies from Arabia, Chinese foxes and Australian Poppykettle gnomes.

You will be transported to mysterious places far beyond our familiar shores – the vanished Atlantis, the elusive Fountain of Youth, King Arthur's dream city of Camelot – and can look into the unknown by consulting an oracle or by studying the position of the stars.

The magical power of witches and wizards extends to the four corners of the earth. In European folktales they fly through the air on broomsticks, bewitch people by the Evil Eye, cast spells and turn themselves into animals. In other parts of the world witch doctors make magic to bring rain for a good harvest, heal the sick and raise the dead.

Throughout history people have believed in all kinds of magical creatures and supernatural beings. We know of them now through the myths and legends that have been passed down over many centuries from generation to generation.

Molly Perham

Greece

The ancient Greeks worshipped many gods and goddesses. Although these beings were all-powerful, they behaved in many ways like ordinary people. The Greeks also believed that all sorts of things and places had their own special spirits. There were spirits of the woods, of mountains, of brooks and fountains, and of the sea. Many of the spirits had human form, but there were also various creatures that were half man and half beast. The Greek Myths are the stories that were told about these gods and spirits.

FAUNS

▷ Fauns were the subjects of Pan, the god of the woods. They used their flutes to help him cause panic (fear of Pan) in humans who strayed across his path.

Fauns are said to be spirits that are part human and part beast. They are sometimes confused with Pan, but are prettier and more graceful. A faun has the body and face of a handsome youth, and the legs, tail and ears of a deer. Unlike satyrs, fauns are gentle creatures. Nymphs and fauns can often be seen dancing together at twilight.

PAN

In Greek mythology, Pan is the god of the woodlands. He has the body and face of a man, but the legs and hooves of a goat. Pan roams around the countryside attended by satyrs and fauns. He likes to chase nymphs, the female spirits of the fields and woods. One of them, Syrinx, was fleeing from him when the virgin

goddess Artemis, to help her escape, changed her into a tuft of reeds. Pan cut some of the reeds and made them into pipes, which he plays as he wanders around. Now, when Greek shepherds hear the wind sighing through the rushes, they say it is Pan playing his pipes.

NYMPHS

N ymphs are the ancient Greek spirits of nature. The singing and dancing of these beautiful maidens is often confused with the ripple of a stream, or a soft breeze through the leaves of a tree. Nymphs are generally shy of humans, but sometimes they carry off handsome young men to live with them.

There are several different kinds of nymphs. Dryads and hamadryads are tree nymphs: they die if the trees in which they live are destroyed. Oreads are the nymphs of mountains and grottos, who guide travellers to their destination.

Naiads preside over brooks and fountains. Nereids are sea nymphs, found in the Mediterranean. They spend most of their time gambolling through the waves with the dolphins and tritons. Oreads, naiads and nereids are all immortal.

TRITONS

T ritons are mermen who accompany the chariot of Poseidon, God of the Ocean. Blowing shrill blasts on conch shells, they warn everyone to keep out of the way. Tritons have scales on their bodies, and fish-like tails that they can change to legs to walk on the land. Whenever they go ashore, they behave very badly and get drunk.

◁◁ Pan once challenged Apollo, the god of music, to a musical contest. Pan played his pipes and Apollo played the lyre, which he had invented. Apollo won the competition by underhand means.

CENTAURS

According to ancient legend, there lived in the mountains of Greece creatures who had the body of a horse, but the chest and head of a human – they were known as centaurs. They were the children of Ixion, one of the Titans, and Nephele, a woman whom the gods made out of a cloud.

The centaurs were wild and savage, and waged war with the Lapiths, a people of a part of Greece called Thessaly, and with the great hero Hercules. They quarrelled with him after one of them entertained him and gave him wine to drink. Most of the centaurs were killed in fights or by the Lapiths.

But not all of the centaurs were so brutish and unruly. One centaur, called Cheiron, was different from his fellows. He was wise and just. Instructed by Apollo, the god of music, and Artemis his sister, who was the goddess of the moon and of hunters, he became known for his skill in hunting, medicine, music and the art of prophecy.

He kept a sort of school where many of the famous Greek heroes were trained, among them Jason and Achilles. When Cheiron died, Zeus placed him among the stars as the constellation Sagittarius.

DIONYSUS

When he was worshipped in Greece thousands of years ago, Dionysus was the god of the powers in nature which make all sorts of plants grow, and allow men and beasts to have offspring. He discovered how to make wine with the grapes that grew on Mount Nysa and became very drunk. He then became known as the god of wine and merriment, and was more often called by the name of Bacchus.

Dionysus, or Bacchus, rode around on a wild ass accompanied by a train of merry followers – satyrs, centaurs and nymphs. Whoever welcomed him kindly received the gift of the vine, but he inflicted dreadful punishments on those who refused to worship him.

Bacchus was worshipped at very wild festivals called Bacchanalia. At these ceremonies, men and women danced and ran about on the hills until they worked themselves up into a kind of madness.

SATYRS

The satyrs are deities of the woods and fields. They have short, sprouting horns and their bodies are covered with bristly hairs. Their legs, hooves and tail are those of a goat. These creatures of the wilderness are rough bullies, and they delight in chasing nymphs, terrifying travellers and frightening sheep. Satyrs always accompany the god Bacchus as he reels around the countryside on his wild ass.

Fairies of Europe

People have believed in fairies from very early times. It may be that some of the earliest inhabitants of Europe were smallish, dark people who lived more or less underground and fled to the woods when the taller invaders occupied their land.

The Little People, as they were called, were thought to have magical powers. As they had their own cattle they probably were skilled in doctoring animals, as well as in poisoning people they disliked. The flint arrowheads made by early men, and still found today, are called elf arrows.

▷ Fairies are said to come in all sizes from small enough to ride a mouse, to full human size. One of the fairy rulers, Queen Mab, is said to have had a chariot carved out of a nutshell.

Folklore says that fairies are supernatural beings, able to interfere magically in the lives of humans. Fairy magic is known as 'glamour'. It operates through a kind of thought power that mortals cannot understand.

Fairies can be seen by horses, dogs and cats, but not usually by humans, unless they choose to show themselves using their magical power – or if there is a full moon on Midsummer Eve, when they have dances and celebrations. Another way of penetrating fairy disguises is to touch your eyes with fairy ointment, as the midwife does in *The Fairy Nurse* (see page 26).

Fairies are like miniature people, though some can change their size and shape at will. They wear red pointed hats, green mantles and pantaloons, and silver shoes. Fairy queens and their attendants wear dresses woven from spider silk and spangled with dew drops. They

often reveal themselves with gossamer wings, to conform with human beliefs, but they don't really need them for flying because they have the power of levitation.

Some fairies are solitary, others are social and live in troops inside hollow hills or in great mounds of earth. Animals are always careful not to trouble the fairies, but humans sometimes go blundering through a fairy market without even seeing it, or tramp noisily over a hill containing a community of fairies. Then they are punished suitably: the punishments range from bad dreams to curses (see *Fair Janet and Tam Lin* on page 18).

Troop fairies are ruled by a fairy queen, who gives out the various tasks. A task may be beneficial to humans, such as making sure that a farmer's cow gives creamy milk, or mischievous, such as stopping the church bells ringing on Sunday morning.

Fairies are curious about human affairs and will often take something away to examine it – then put it back in the wrong place. They are very interested in romances, and if they approve will do anything they can to help the couple. But if they feel a

couple are unsuited, they will do what they can to break them up.

A fairy godmother usually appears in a house soon after the birth of a baby. She bestows various gifts on the child, such as beauty or cleverness – or if the fairy has been offended in some way, ugliness or a physical disability. Fairies sometimes will steal a baby, leaving their own in its place, or they lead humans away to Fairyland to act as midwives (see *The Fairy Nurse*).

A cross is the most powerful protection against fairies, as it is against all evil spirits. This might be the sign of a cross, a wooden cross, a cross worn round the neck or even a crossroads, as in *Fair Janet and Tam Lin*. Mothers would sometimes protect their babies from the fairies by hanging a pair of open scissors, in the shape of a cross, above the cradle.

NIXIES

I n the old legends of Germany, water fairies are called nixies. Male nixies rarely show themselves, but they look the same as humans, except

that they have green teeth, and they wear green hats.

Female nixies are very beautiful creatures. They sit on the river banks combing their long fair hair. If a handsome young man stops to admire them, they lure him down into the water and he is never seen again.

The females go to human markets to do their shopping, very neatly dressed, but can be recognized because some part of their clothing – the corner of an apron or the hem of a skirt – is always sopping wet. Human midwives are often called to assist nixie mothers.

◁ One of the most famous nixies was the Lorelei. She was said to have been the daughter of the River Rhine. The story goes that she lived on a rock in the middle of the Rhine and lured many young men to their deaths. They fell from its sheer sides trying to reach her. She was finally defeated by two old mountaineers who climbed the rock and threatened her with their guns. She called on her father for help and was swept away by a great wave, never to be seen again. However the Lorelei Rock can still be seen if you cruise up the Rhine.

Fair Janet and Tam Lin

Tam Lin and Fair Janet were the children of two Scottish earls. They loved each other from childhood, but when the time came for their marriage, Tam Lin vanished. No one knew what had happened to him.

Many days after Tam Lin disappeared, Fair Janet went walking in Carterhaugh Wood, though she had been warned not to go there. She wandered between the trees and bushes picking flowers, and had just plucked a wild rose when Tam Lin suddenly appeared at her side.

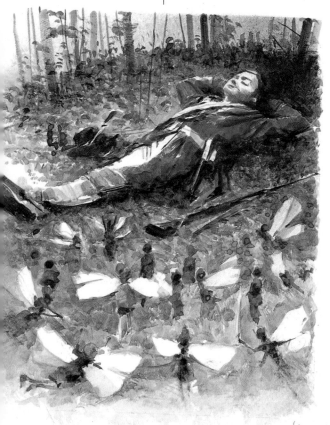

'Where have you come from?' cried Janet. 'And why have you been away for so long?'

'I come from Fairyland,' said Tam Lin. 'I was out hunting on that mound over there when I was overcome with drowsiness and fell asleep. When I woke, I was in Fairyland. The queen of the fairies has made me her knight. It's a good place to be, but for one thing. Every seven years the fairies must make a sacrifice to the Underworld, and although the queen is good to me, I fear that I am to be that sacrifice.'

When she heard this dreadful news Fair Janet begged to know how she could help Tam Lin.

'There is only one way of saving me,' said Tam Lin. 'Tomorrow night is Hallowe'en, and the Fairy Court will ride right through Scotland. Stand by the pool at Miles Cross at midnight and sprinkle holy water all around you. I will be riding on a milk-white horse at the Queen's side. Look at my hands, Janet, and you will see that the right one will be gloved and the left one bare.

'You must spring on me as I pass, and I will fall to the ground. Then, whatever happens, hold on to me tightly until they turn me into a red-hot iron blade. Throw the blade into the pool and I will become a man again.'

The next night Fair Janet waited at Miles Cross until the Fairy Court came riding over the mound. As soon as she saw the milk-white horse, she seized the bridle and pulled its rider to the ground.

All the fairies gathered round and cast their spells on Tam Lin. First they made him into a block of ice in Janet's arms, and then into a roaring flame. The fire vanished and she was holding a snake that reared up as if to bite her. Next they turned the snake into a dove that struggled to fly away. But

Janet held on, until at last he was turned into a red-hot blade. Janet quickly threw the blade into the pool and Tam Lin became a man again.

With mournful cries, the Fairy Court rode away. Fair Janet and Tam Lin went home together and were married soon after.

BOGGARTS
GREMLINS
BOGIES ←
LEPRECHAUNS   TROLLS ←
BROWNIES   HOBGOBLINS
GOBLINS
PIXIES
ELVES
FAIRIES   GNOMES

BANNICK

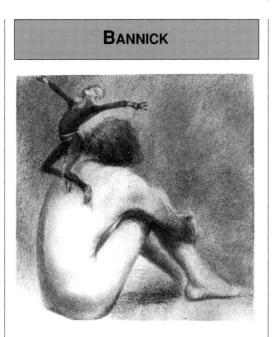

The bannick is a spirit of the bath house. They used to live only in Russia and Scandinavia, flitting about in the hot steam from the sauna. But now that sauna baths are popular in other parts of the world, bannicks can be found elsewhere. A bannick caress on your back is a good omen; a scratch signifies misfortune.

BOGGART

A boggart is a house spirit. Rather like a poltergeist, he makes his home with a chosen family and then persecutes them, doing all kinds of things to make their lives unbearable. Sometimes he walks through the bedrooms at night, pulling the covers off sleeping people, or knocks loudly at the door and never comes in or answers. Sometimes he rearranges the furniture so that people bump into it. Boggarts particularly enjoy teasing children by snatching away their food or shoving them into cupboards.

One farmer's family was particularly plagued by a boggart. The children didn't mind this as much as the adults. They enjoyed taunting the boggart by thrusting sticks into an elf-bore – the hole where a knot of wood has been – and then dodging as the boggart shot them back.

However, the boggart's tricks got worse and eventually the farmer decided to move. Just as he was packing his cart with all the family's possessions a voice came out of the butter churn, and he realized that there was no escape, for the boggart was moving with them.

BENDITH Y MAMAU

Unlike true fairies, who are noted for their beauty, the Welsh Bendith y Mamau of legend are horrible, stunted, little creatures. They are always stealing human children and leaving their own ugly offspring, called crimbils, in exchange. However a parent can usually get their child back with the help of a wise man or woman.

◁ The Bendith y Mamau are said to steal children who can walk and talk, unlike the true fairies who only take babies. When the child returns to its family, it can remember nothing of its experience except listening to sweet music.

DWARVES

oremasters describe the dwarves as a race of small men and women with malformed bodies and big heads. They have the power to make themselves invisible, usually by means of an enchanted cap or cloak, which they will sometimes lend to mere mortals. Although wary of humans, they are generally friendly, but if provoked they can be vindictive and mischievous.

Dwarves live underground and are skilful miners and metal workers. Spears and swords made by them always find their mark and often protect their owners.

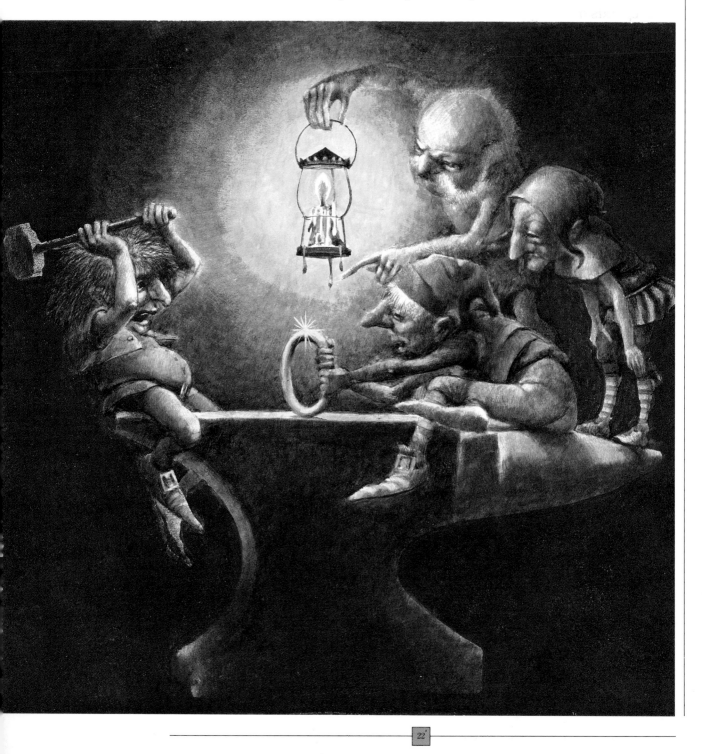

However, these things have to be gifts and cannot be bought. Misfortune will befall anyone who steals a dwarf weapon or takes it by force. Dwarves are said to be savage fighters when provoked. They use axes in preference to any other weapon, and wear coats of mail for protection.

Dwarves are often mentioned in the legends of Europe. A knight who was lucky enough to possess a suit of armour made by a dwarf was always kept safe in any fight. Germany is said to be the principal home of the dwarves, though they also live in Scandinavia and in the Swiss mountains.

BODACH

n the Scottish Highlands, a house spirit is called a bodach. During the day, he lives up the chimney, listening for troublesome children who make a fuss at bedtime. When they have eventually gone to bed he comes down the chimney and pulls their noses and ears. Then he gives the children nightmares by lifting up their eyelids and scowling into

their eyes. A pinch of salt sprinkled on the fire before going to bed will keep the bodach at bay.

CLURICAUNE

The cluricaune is one of the solitary fairies of Ireland. He wears a red coat and cap, and lives in the cellars of inns and houses. Normally cluricaunes cause no trouble, but if the householder is too fond of his drink, a cluricaune will also consume large quantities of wine and even break the bottles. Sometimes he causes so much trouble that the householder moves; but the cluricaune pops into a cask and moves with him.

GNOMES

Gnomes live underground, guarding the treasures of the earth. They are not miners like the dwarves, but they know where all the coal, gold, silver and precious stones are hidden. Each group or family of gnomes looks after a particular vein of gold or seam of coal.

◁ The best way to get rid of an annoying cluricaune is to cut off his supply of drink. Then the cluricane will move elsewhere in search of a more generous household.

If gnomes come above ground at all, they choose the dusk and evening to do their travelling so that they are less likely to be seen. Like cats and owls, their eyes are adapted to seeing in the dark.

Gnomes are very good-humoured, and because they lead peaceful lives and never worry about anything they live for hundreds of years. They are also helpful to humans, and often guide prospectors towards the riches under the ground. However, some clumsy miners wreck entire colonies of these little people, and then the gnomes turn against them and make things difficult by pulling away pit props or diverting underground streams.

As more and more mines have been dug, some gnomes have migrated to the forests, where they have established colonies among the roots of large trees. Now that humans have felled so many of the forests, gnomes find it more and more difficult to find places to live.

GOBLINS

G oblins are said to have a human form, but are small and rather grotesque. Like fairies, elves and pixies, they are spirits of the earth. But unlike the other spirits, goblins are usually malicious.

Goblins originally came from France, and then spread all over Europe, sailing to Britain on Viking ships. French mothers used to threaten naughty children that 'the goblin will eat you; the goblin will take you away'. Stealing children is one of their nastier tricks, and they also torment humans by tipping over pails of milk, hiding hens' eggs, blowing soot down chimneys, and snuffing out candles.

Hobgoblins are not as evil as goblins, just rather mischievous. Some Cornish goblins, or buccas, are really quite friendly. The Cornish tin mine spirits, called knockers, knock to tell the miners where ore can be found, or to warn them of impending disasters.

When Cornish miners emigrated to Australia to work in the copper mines they discovered that there were knockers there, too. In Australia they are known as knackers. Goblins also inhabit gold and silver mines in other parts of the world. They can often be heard working with pickaxes and hammers, doing the same work that the miners do.

ROBIN GOODFELLOW

obin Goodfellow is the most famous of the hobgoblins. He was half fairy and half human. His father was Oberon, and his mother a pretty country girl whom the fairy king fell in love with. Robin was brought up by his mother, but when he was six years old Oberon gave him the power to change his shape whenever he needed to help or punish mortals.

The Fairy Nurse

Near Coolgarrow in Ireland there lived a farmer called Michael, with his wife Molly and three small children, the youngest of them newly born. Molly was a good wife and mother, but she was so busy that she often neglected to say her prayers. One Sunday morning she was even late for church, because she had stopped to consult a fairy man (a local wise man) about a sick cow.

In the middle of that night, Michael was woken by the baby crying, and when he sat up and lit a lamp, he saw that Molly was no longer by his side. The children told him that the room had been full of little people dressed in white, red and green. They had seen their mother in the middle of them, going out of the door as if she was walking in her sleep.

The farmer searched everywhere for his wife, but could not find her. The children became neglected and dirty, and the baby had to be put out to nurse. Then one morning, a neighbour who was also a midwife came up to him and said, 'I have some news of your Molly.

'Last night, just as I was falling asleep, there was a knock at the door. When I went downstairs there was a dark gentleman mounted on a black horse. He lifted me up behind him, and before I realized what had happened, we were in front of a big castle. We went into a great hall, painted in red and gold, with fine carpets and furniture. Then we came to a room where a beautiful lady was lying in bed, and I helped her to have her baby.

'The dark gentleman gave me a jar of green ointment and told me to rub the baby all over with it. But as I was rubbing, my eye began to itch and I scratched it with my finger. Suddenly the room changed before my very eyes to a cave with water running through it. The fine gentleman and lady, and the baby, became poor thin creatures dressed in old rags.

'I went on rubbing the baby as if nothing had happened, and after a while the gentleman told me to go and wait in the hall and he would take me home. And that is when Molly came in, looking pale and frightened. She told me that we were inside the green hill that stands outside the village. The lady who has just given birth was the queen of the fairies, and Molly is to be the child's nurse.'

The farmer turned pale when he heard this. 'But when will we see her again?' he asked in despair. 'We need her at home with her own children.'

'All is not lost,' the midwife reassured him. 'Once a month, on the night of the full moon, a door opens in the side of the hill. On that night, you must go to the hill carrying a cockerel hidden under your coat, a piece of iron, and a Bible to defend yourself against the wrath of the fairy people.

'When the door opens, wedge it wide with the piece of iron. Then you must go inside, grab your wife by the waist and hold her tight, because the fairies will do their best to try and stop you from rescuing her.'

So, at the next full moon, Michael gathered up an iron sickle, a cockerel and his Bible and went to the green hill. Just as the midwife had said, a door opened. He stuck his sickle into the door post to stop it closing while he was inside the hill. Then he put the cockerel under his coat and stepped boldly in.

He found himself in the great hall of a castle. It was full of people, but at the far end he spied

Molly nursing the baby. When he started to make his way through the crowd to her, several of the fairies grabbed at him to try and stop him.

But he clasped the Bible firmly to his chest and forged on. As the farmer got closer to his stolen wife, the fairies jostled him more and more. In the tussle, the cockerel escaped and instantly crowed loudly. The fairies drew back, startled. They thought dawn had come and the hillside door was still open. Any passing mortal could see the door and invade their land.

In the mad confusion that followed, Michael lunged forward and caught Molly around the waist. He dragged her towards the door. As they stepped into the open air, there was thunder and lightning all around and ugly figures grasped at them out of the mists. But the farmer held his wife tight and made the sign of the cross at the looming monsters. At that, the sickle was thrown after them and the door in the hillside slammed shut.

At last everything was quiet, and Molly lay fainting in her husband's arms. He carried her home to her children, and from then on she always made time to say her prayers, and never took advice from a fairy man again. Nor did the fairies try to take their revenge on Michael or his family.

A few weeks later, the midwife saw the dark gentleman again. He was stealing butter from a stall at the local market. To her surprise, no one seemed to notice what he was doing, or even to see that he was there.

The midwife went up to him and touched his arm. 'Sir,' she said, 'I hope your lady is well, and the baby is thriving.'

'Both are very well, thank you,' he replied. 'And how do you think I look in this new suit?'

'I can't see you with my eye on that side,' she said.

So he struck her on her Seeing Eye with his riding crop, blinding the eye, and she could never see the fairies again.

PIXIES

According to the old tales, pixies are homelier in appearance than fairies. They are easily recognized by their pointed ears, turned-up noses and round faces. They have red hair and green eyes, and dress in green tunics and pointed green caps. Pixies live in south-western England, especially in Cornwall.

Pixies, like hobgoblins, are mischievous spirits. They play all kinds of practical jokes on humans who live near them, such as stealing horses out of the stable at night and bringing them home in the morning sweating and exhausted. A farmer will nail an old horseshoe over the stable door to prevent his horses being taken away.

In particular pixies enjoy leading travellers astray. The only way you can save yourself from being pixy-led is to turn your coat inside out.

If pixies take up residence in your house, a gift of clothes will encourage them to leave. And if they are being really troublesome, the sound of church bells will drive them away.

An old folk tale tells of a farmer from Knighton who was very friendly with the pixies. In the evenings he would leave a pile of corn in the barn and they would thrash it for him. One night the farmer's wife peeped through a crack in the barn door and saw the pixies working hard, but was horrified to see that they were wearing no clothes. She thought it was a terrible shame that they should be naked and cold, and set to work to make some clothes for them. She left the clothes on the threshing floor, and after that the pixies did not come again.

Some time afterwards new bells were hung in the local church. The pixy father came to see the farmer and asked if he could borrow his horse and cart. The farmer had heard how pixies use horses, so he was rather reluctant and asked what the pixy wanted them for.

'I want to take my wife and children away from the noise of the bells,' the pixy explained.

So the farmer lent his horse and cart and the pixies moved away over the hill to the next village. And when the old horse trotted back home he was as fresh as a young colt.

◁ Pixies are very fond of music and have been known to lead a good musician to buried treasure. However, they punish bad players by confusing them and leading them into bogs and briar patches.

GREMLIN EFFECT (GE)

ANALYSIS USING THE 'MAGIC' ODIN-RUNIC
CALIBRATION BY GREM-LINES

CALCULATED BY
Pilot-Officer Prune — Royal Air Force.   DATE

GREMLINS

Almost all fairies have been around since time began, but the gremlins are a new race that revealed itself only in this century. Airforce pilots were the first people to come across the gremlins: an engine that was perfectly all right the night before failed to start; or there was an unaccountable leakage of petrol from the tanks, or air from the tyres. Sightings have been made at different locations in various parts of the world, but it is generally agreed that there is a horde of malicious spirits whose sole purpose is to bring about all those little mishaps that plague our lives.

Gremlins lurk around anyone who is using tools or machinery. So if you have ever wondered why there is always a knot in a plank of wood just where you want to saw, or why the sewing thread always runs out just before you have got to the end of a seam – blame it on the gremlins!

KOBOLDS

German house spirits are called kobolds. These little old men are much more useful than boggarts and bodachs because they work extremely hard. They actually enjoy cleaning and sweeping, washing dishes, and carrying water. They work outdoors too, milking the cows, grooming the horses, collecting eggs, or chopping wood. Kobolds live on scraps left over from the dinner table and dishes of milk or cream, but if a housewife forgets to feed them, they will take their revenge. She will break dishes, lose her purse or her favourite clothes, burn her fingers, or fall downstairs.

LEPRECHAUNS

Leprechauns are the best-known fairies of the Irish legends, and unlike other spirits they are visible to humans. People who have seen them say that they are dressed in green, with a red cap, buckled shoes and a leather apron. The apron is the uniform of their trade, for leprechauns are cobblers, making shoes for all the other fairies.

▽ Leprechauns are said to keep their gold in a pottery jar. If you can catch one, he must show you where it is hidden. However, many people have gone leprechaun hunting and very few have become rich! It is better to leave them alone.

The Arabian Nights is a collection of stories told by Queen Scheherazade to her husband King Shahriman over a period of a thousand and one nights. Arab people were firm believers in the influence of good and evil spirits on the human race. Genies, or jinns, were able to assume human or animal form. A perie was a good genie, endowed with grace and beauty. One of the tales in *The Arabian Nights* tells how the perie Maimunah and a disreputable genie called Dahnash had a bet on whose beauty was greater, that of Prince Kamar al-Zaman, or Princess Budur.

Prince Kamar al-Zaman and Princess Budur

There was once a sultan called Shahriman, who ruled over the land of Khalidan. Shahriman had many wives and all the riches that he could wish for, but he was childless and this made him very sad. Then, when Shahriman was very old and had given up all hope of having a child, his newest and youngest wife gave birth to a son.

The baby was so beautiful that his father called him Kamar al-Zaman, moon of the time. As the boy became older he grew even more beautiful, and eventually the time came when Shahriman wanted to find him a wife.

The sultan called Kamar al-Zaman to him and said, 'My son, I would like to see you married during my lifetime. I look forward to celebrating your wedding to a suitable princess.'

Kamar al-Zaman turned pale when he heard his father's words. 'But Father,' he said, 'I have no wish to get married. I don't like women. I have read a great deal about their wickedness and deceit. Even at the risk of upsetting you, I would not hesitate to kill myself if you forced me into marriage.'

The sultan was very upset by his son's reply, but he loved him so much that he said, 'I do not wish to force you, if the prospect is so disagreeable. You are still young, and will have time to reflect and consider how happy I would be to see you married and the father of children.'

For a whole year Shahriman spoke no more about the subject, but at the end of that time he called his son to him again and said, 'Have you thought about what I said, and the happiness that your marriage would bring me?'

But Kamar al-Zaman replied, 'I have thought about marriage for a whole year and read many books on the subject. I am convinced that women are foolish and disgusting, and that death would be better than have anything to do with them.'

Shahriman realized that it would be useless to force his son to obey him, so he discussed the problem with his grand vizier, who thought for a long time before answering. 'Be patient for another year,' he advised, 'and then, instead of talking to your son in secret, announce your intention of finding him a bride in front of the whole court. He is sure to obey you in front of so many people.'

So the sultan waited for another year and then summoned his son before the assembled court. 'My son,' he said, 'I have brought you here in the presence of all these gentlemen to tell you that I am about to marry you to a suitable princess.'

Kamar al-Zaman was so horrified that for the first time in his life he was rude to his father. The sultan, unable to ignore such public insolence, ordered the guards to take the boy and shut him up in an old ruined tower near the palace. One of the guards stayed at the door of the prison to watch over the prince and attend to his needs.

At the back of the tower there was a well which was the home of a young perie called Maimunah. She was the daughter of Dimiryat, king of the subterranean genies, and was known for her power and virtue. Towards midnight Maimunah left the well to take the air and as she passed the top of the tower she was surprised to see a light in a place that had been so long neglected.

'There must be some reason for this light,' she said to herself. 'I will go and see.'

Swerving in her flight, she entered the tower and passed over the sleeping body of the guard into Kamar al-Zaman's bedchamber. The prince was asleep, and did not wake although Maimunah stayed there for a whole hour admiring his beauty.

'How can the parents of this lovely boy be so cruel as to shut him in a tower,' she thought. 'Do they not know about the wicked genies who haunt ruins? I will take him under my protection and guard him from any genie who tries to harm him.'

As Maimunah was leaving the tower she heard a furious beating of wings and recognized Dahnash, a vulgar genie who was the son of Shamhurish, the swiftest flyer. She was so afraid that Dahnash might see the light in the tower that she swooped down on him like a sparrowhawk and was about to dash him to the ground when he made a sign of surrender. Then he told her of his adventure.

'I have just come from Ghayyur the Great's lands beyond the farthest reaches of China, and I have never seen anyone as beautiful as his only daughter, Princess Budur. Her face is as white as snow and her hair falls in dark rivers to the floor. Her cheeks are flushed like a rose, and her lips as red as cherries.

'The king loves his daughter so much that he built seven magnificent palaces for her, each of a different material. The first is entirely of crystal, the second of alabaster, the third of porcelain, the fourth of stone mosaics, the fifth of silver, the sixth of gold and the seventh of diamonds.

'Many princes have sought the hand of this beautiful princess, but she has rejected them all. I go every night to look at her beauty while she sleeps. Come with me, Maimunah, and see for yourself. Her loveliness will amaze you!'

When Dahnash had finished, Maimunah burst out laughing. 'You have seen nothing,' she said scornfully. 'No beauty could compare with that of the handsome youth I have just left.'

'Pardon me,' said Dahnash sarcastically. 'Who is this youth and where is he?'

'He is shut in the old tower behind which I live. I will take you to see him, and I will expect you to pay a large forfeit if my prince is more beautiful than your princess.'

So the two of them entered Kamar al-Zaman's chamber and Dahnash looked at the sleeping youth.

'I can see why you think your friend is incomparable,' he said thoughtfully, 'because I too have never seen such a beautiful boy. But I can assure you that the mould he was made in has cast a female copy also.'

Maimunah gave Dahnash such a violent blow about his head with her wing that one of his horns broke.

'You horrible genie!' she screamed. 'I order you to go at once to the palace of this Budur and bring her back with you. When you return, we will compare the two.'

Dahnash flew off at the speed of light and returned within the hour with the sleeping princess on his shoulders. He laid her down on the bed next to Kamar al-Zaman, and Maimunah was forced to admit that they could be twins, so similar was their beauty.

'We will see who can compose the most beautiful verses in praise of their favourite,' she suggested. And so they did, but still neither of them was proved the winner.

'There is only one way to end this dispute,' said Maimunah, 'and that is to refer it to a third party.'

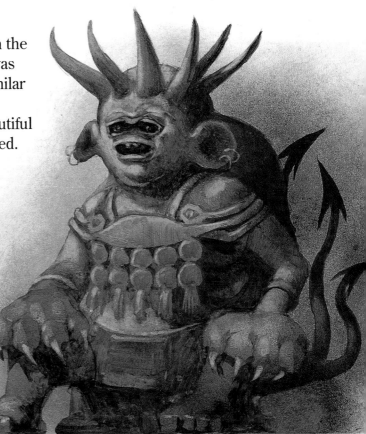

She stamped hard on the floor and it opened to reveal the ugliest genie imaginable. He was humpbacked and lame, and had three forked tails. On his head were six horns, and his eyes were where his nose should be. His hands were as large as cauldrons, with claws like a lion. His name was Kashkash ibn Fakrash ibn Atrash.

Kashkash regarded the two young people sleeping and said, 'As Allah lives, they are equal in beauty. Their difference is one of sex alone. Wake one after the other, while we three remain invisible. The one who shows the greater love will lose the contest, by finding the charms of the other more irresistible.'

Maimunah and Dahnash thought this was an excellent idea, so Dahnash changed himself into a flea and bit Kamar al-Zaman on the neck. The youth woke with a start, and his eyes fell on the beautiful girl beside him. But just as he was about to kiss her a thought came to him.

'My father has placed this girl in my bed,' he said to himself, 'so that tomorrow he can accuse me of being a liar and trickster.'

To Maimunah's delight, the prince turned his back and went back to sleep. Then she turned herself into a flea and bit Budur's thigh.

The princess gave a cry of terror and astonishment when she saw such a beautiful young man lying beside her. She leaned over and kissed him, but Kamar al-Zaman was kept in a deep sleep by Maimunah, and did not respond to Budur's affection.

The three genies had watched all this, and Maimunah was delighted to have proved to Dahnash that he had lost his wager. She told him to take the princess back to the palace of King Ghayyur, and then they went off in different directions.

Determined to marry the beautiful unknown each had seen in a dream, Prince Kamar al-Zaman and Princess Budur eventually found each other after many trials and adventures. They married and lived happily ever after.

Miss Jen

According to Chinese folklore, at the age of fifty a fox can shape-shift into a woman. At the age of a hundred, it can change into a beautiful girl, or a wizard. It can know about happenings a thousand li distant (1 li = 545 metres), and it can bewitch people, leading them astray and causing them to lose their wits. At the age of a thousand, a fox can communicate with heaven. *Miss Jen* is a tale from the T'ang dynasty in China.

Wei Yin was the grandson of the Prince of Hsin-an, while Hsuan Cheng was so poor that he had no home of his own and lived with his mother's relations. Despite their different circumstances, Yin and Cheng were the best of friends.

One day they were going to a feast together when Cheng excused himself saying he would join Yin later. While Yin turned eastwards on his white horse, Cheng went south on his donkey.

Three women were walking in that street. Cheng thought that one, dressed in white, was particularly beautiful. He began to follow them, and the woman in white kept looking back as if she was aware of his attentions.

'Such a beautiful lady should not be walking in the streets of Ch'ang-an,' said Cheng jokingly.

'Well if some people who are mounted will not lend their beast, what am I to do?' the lady replied.

'A donkey is hardly fit to carry a lady,' said Cheng. 'But have mine if you want to, and I will be happy to follow on foot.'

Soon Cheng was on familiar terms with the ladies and he followed them to the Pleasure Gardens, where they stopped outside a gate in a mud wall. Behind the gate was an imposing residence, and Cheng was invited inside. The lady introduced herself as Miss Jen, and they dined together and had a merry evening. Next day Cheng asked a shopkeeper whose house it was behind the mud wall, and the man said, 'It is all waste land behind the wall. There is a fox there who lures men to her lair. I have seen it happen three times. I suppose you, too, have been enticed by her?'

Cheng was too ashamed to admit this, and when Yin reproached him for not keeping his appointment he lied about it. Nevertheless, he remembered Miss Jen's charms and when he saw her again he begged her to set up house with him. Cheng asked his friend to loan some furniture, and Yin sent his servant to spy on the couple. The servant reported back that Cheng was living with the most beautiful woman in all the world.

Curious to see who it could be, Yin went to Cheng's house and found Miss Jen alone. As soon as he saw how lovely she was Yin tried to force her to submit to him, but Miss Jen struggled to repel him.

'How can you do this to your friend,' she asked reproachfully. 'You are rich and have enjoyed the love of many beautiful women. Cheng is poor and I am his only delight.'

When he heard this Yin released Miss Jen and admitted that he had been at fault. Soon afterwards Cheng came in, and from then on Yin supplied everything the couple needed. Yin and Miss Jen became good friends, and she took it upon herself to arrange meetings with any lady that he fancied. After about a year Cheng was appointed Deputy Military Officer in another province. He asked Miss Jen to accompany him to his new posting, but at first she refused, saying that a sorceress had warned her against journeying in that year. Cheng dismissed her fears and eventually persuaded her to go with him. They journeyed for two days. Miss Jen rode her horse in front, Cheng rode on his donkey behind her, followed by her maid on another mount. The weather was fine and they made good time.

As they reached Ma-wei they passed a groom who was training his hounds for the hunt. The dogs rushed out of the long grass, and in that instant Cheng saw Miss Jen fall from her horse, turn into a fox, and run off towards the south. The dogs chased after their prey, and after only one li, caught up with the fox and killed it.

With tears in his eyes, Cheng buried the dead fox, marking the spot with a wooden stick planted in the earth. The horse grazed by the side of the road, with Miss Jen's clothes on the saddle and her shoes in the stirrups.

WANDJINAS

In Dreamtime, the time before the Aborigines lived in Australia, the land was occupied by the spirit ancestors of all the people, plants and animals living there now. These spirits created the elements and control the weather and the land.

The Wandjinas control the climate and the fertility of the land. They live inside the mountains of northern Australia, and emerge only when it is time to change the seasons from wet to dry or back.

Wandjinas look like humans, but are three times as large. The strange thing about them is that they have no mouths. If they did, every time they opened their mouths they would release all the weather that is stored inside their bodies. This would upset the seasonal pattern of the climate and cause perpetual rain.

▽ One of the strangest things about the Wandjinas is their strange, space-helmet type of headdress. It has led people to wonder if they first came from outer space.

ABATWA

The tiniest fairies of all are said to be even smaller than ants. In fact the Abatwa of southern Africa actually live in ant hills, sharing their home with the ants and foraging for food among the roots of grasses and other plants.

The Abatwa look exactly like native Africans and live like them in tribes and family clans. They are shy little creatures and like to be

left in peace. The only humans who ever see the Abatwa are small children and women who are expecting babies. If a woman in the seventh month of pregnancy sees a male Abatwa she knows that she will give birth to a son.

URBAR DRUM

The rainy season has always been very important for the crop growers of northern Australia, and various rituals are performed to make sure that it arrives on time. As part of these rituals a drum is

carved out of a hollow log, and the Aborigines re-enact the making of the first drum.

Jurawadbad the python-man was betrothed to an Aborigine girl called Mimaliwu, but she allowed herself to be seduced by a water snake. Jurawadbad was so angry that he made an urbar, or drum, and hid inside it. When Mimaliwu and her mother reached inside the urbar searching for honey or grubs to eat, the python-man bit them and they died. Their spirits are now associated with the rainy season.

RAINFOREST GNOMES

Gnomes are generally helpful creatures, and the ones that live in the tropical rainforests of northern Queensland in Australia are no exception. Because of the humid climate, the green tree frogs get nasty croak infections. The forest gnomes are kept busy applying a special linctus to the frogs' tonsils. They do this with a large swab tied onto the end of a broom handle.

Poppykettle Gnomes

In 1847 two men were digging for lime in the cliffs near Geelong in Victoria, Australia. One of their shovels clinked against metal and they unearthed two ancient brass keys. Nobody could understand how the keys came to be buried so deep in the ground. The Aborigines did not use keys, and the white settlers had been in Australia for only a very short time. This is the story of how the keys got there.

Many years ago, after the Spanish adventurers had sailed across the ocean and conquered the people of Peru, seven Inca gnomes decided to set off and see what lay beyond the horizon to the west.

A brown pelican carried the gnomes to the city of Machu Picchu high in the Andes Mountains. There they found a clay pot with a spout and a handle, and decided it would be the ideal craft for their voyage.

The great Silverado Bird carried the pot and its crew down to the seashore, where the gnomes made a sail and winched on board two brass keys, which they had stolen from the Spaniards, to provide ballast. They felt this was a fair exchange because the Spanish had stolen so much silver and gold from the the people of Peru.

They also loaded sacks of poppy seed as provisions for the voyage – enough to last them several years. The ship was named *The Poppykettle*.

A silver fish towed *The Poppykettle* through the water until the wind caught the sail and blew the little craft out across the vast Pacific Ocean. They were helped on their way by El Nino, the cosmic power that controls the winds, the ocean and the climate of lands around the Pacific.

After a few days the wind dropped and the gnomes were almost wrecked on some rocky islands, which we know as the Galapagos Islands. However, some great dragon-like monsters filled the sail with their hot breath and drove them out to sea again.

The Poppykettle sailed on for months and months until it was carried close to another island. This time the clay pot was almost shattered on the coral reefs, but the gnomes were rescued by some of the islanders, who showed them a chart to help them find the way on the next stretch of the voyage.

Now the intrepid explorers sailed through rougher and colder waters. The wind gathered force and blew up into a great storm. *The Poppykettle* tossed about on giant waves, and the gnomes feared they would all perish in the swell.

After many hours the gale subsided, but *The Poppykettle*

had cracked and was slowly filling with water. Luckily a
dolphin had followed them through the storm. He lifted the damaged pot
out of the water and carried it on his head, all the way to a far distant shore.

The Inca gnomes left the clay pot and the brass keys on the beach and
set off to explore this Unknown and Unchosen Land. They were the first
gnome settlers in Australia.

Over three hundred years later, in 1847, two men were digging in the
cliffs near Geelong in Victoria. One of them dug out two brass keys – the
very ones that the gnomes had brought all the way from Peru.

Magical Places

Throughout history people have travelled the world in search of paradise and immortality. Tales and legends of dream lands abound in myths and folklore. The ocean depths may one day yield the secrets of once fertile and prosperous lands such as Lyonesse and Atlantis, or someone may stumble across the hidden utopia of Shangri-La, but for the moment these magical places remain a secret.

AVALON

Avalon is a mythical isle in the centre of a great lake, where the sun always shines and there is perfect peace. In the paradise of Avalon heroes are cured of mortal wounds and restored to their youthful vigour.

Merlin the magician took King Arthur to the lake of Avalon after he had lost his sword in a fierce fight. There an arm stretched up out of the water clasping a splendid new one. The sword Excalibur had magical powers, and served Arthur well until his last fatal battle against his wicked nephew Mordred, who was determined to make himself king and marry Queen Guinevere.

When almost all the knights on both sides had been slain in that terrible battle, Mordred and Arthur met and fought. Arthur ran his spear through Mordred's body, but at the moment of his death Mordred struck Arthur and mortally wounded him.

Sir Bedivere carried the dying king to the shores of Lake Avalon, and at Arthur's command threw his mighty sword Excalibur into the water. A hand reached up and drew it under, the same hand that had held it up for Arthur many years before. Then a barge approached over the lake and the Lady of the Lake took Arthur off to have his wounds attended to in Avalon.

Some say that Avalon is Arthur's final resting place, but others think that one day when his country needs him, he will return.

LYONESSE

Tristan, one of the Knights of the Round Table, was the son of King Rivalen of Lyonesse. This island nation was in the Atlantic Ocean, near the Isles of Scilly. It had several towns and a hundred and forty churches. As time went by Lyonesse was engulfed by the ocean, but from Land's End at the south-west tip of Cornwall you can still see where it lay, and hear the church bells tolling mournfully beneath the waves.

Lyonesse was an idyllic island with a perfect climate, much favoured as a resting-place for weary knights and lovesick maidens. The fertile land produced several crops of fruit, vegetables and flowers each year, and the inhabitants were particularly noble and handsome.

CAMELOT

Arthur was a legendary warrior-king who lived in the south-west of Britain about eight hundred years ago. Tales of how he came to the throne, of battles fought and won, and of his court of noble knights and their adventures, have enthralled

▽ Every knight going or returning from a quest, every damsel in distress, every challenge to Arthur's rule of law entered Camelot through the great gate. Merlin himself carved the stone dragons that guarded it.

listeners since medieval times.

Camelot was the dream city which King Arthur made his capital and headquarters. It stood on a hill rising up out of a plain, and was surrounded by mysterious forests. Legend has it that the city was built by the fairies, and their music can still be heard in the stillness before dawn. A traveller to Camelot might just see the spires and turrets of the enchanted castle fading away into the evening twilight.

In the centre of Camelot was the Great Hall, where Arthur held his court and all the knights gathered

once a year to celebrate the Feast of Pentecost. Along the walls of the hall there was a row of shields made of stone, each bearing the name of a knight. A shield remained blank until its owner had done a noble deed, and then Arthur had the knight's name carved on it.

At the end of each day the knights gathered at the Round Table in the Great Hall to hear the tales of the adventures and to celebrate the victories of returning knights. The table was round so that no knight would seem to be more important than another; all were equal in a circle of friendship.

JOYOUS GARDE

One of King Arthur's knights, Sir Lancelot, was looking for a noble deed to prove his knighthood. Arthur set him the task of capturing a castle that was under an evil enchantment. It was a dark and dismal place called Dolorous Garde, meaning Sorrowful Castle, and was occupied by a band of knights who had fallen into evil ways. Lancelot accepted the challenge and attacked the castle single-handed. He drove out the wicked knights and inside the castle he found a tomb with his own name on it. He realized at once that this was his destined burial place.

Lancelot transformed Dolorous Garde into one of the most spectacular castles in the world. The outer walls were gilded with gold leaf, and brightly coloured pennants flew from all the turrets and spires. Inside the walls were hung with brilliant tapestries.

Lancelot renamed the castle Joyous Garde and took Queen Guinevere there when he rescued her from an unjust execution. After Arthur went to Avalon, Lancelot became a hermit. When he died, his body was taken to Joyous Garde and buried in the tomb.

WOODMAN'S HALL

According to an old story, in the forests of northern Europe there is a timber lodge that is the eternal home of hunters. Only good hunters go there – those who have hunted for food, not for the pleasure of killing.

The lodge is a rambling old building that looks as if bits have been added over the years. Smoke rises from the many chimneys, and small windows with panes of green glass look out over a clearing.

Not far from the lodge there is a lake teeming with fish such as pike, carp and trout. Flocks of water birds nest among the reeds. The forest is home to all kinds of wildlife, including bison, wild boar, and bears. During the day the hunters go out to enjoy their sport, but even if animals are caught and killed they are still there on the following day.

SHANGRI-LA

I n a fertile valley called Shangri-La, beyond the western Himalayas, a group of coloured pavilions with blue roofs clings to the hillside. Above them soar the snowy slopes in a dazzling pyramid. In this idyllic setting lives a perfect community of people governed by Buddhist priests, called lamas. There are no strict rules and the people live in peace and harmony with each other. This secret valley is so remote that only a few have been able to find it.

ATLANTIS

A tlantis was an imaginary city in the Atlantic Ocean. It stood on nine circles of land, linked by great bridges to an island in the centre.

◁ The valley of Shangri-La was last visited by a party of Europeans in the 1930s. They were escaping from the unrest in China and were crossing the Himalayas when they stumbled upon this marvellous valley. The people of the valley had discovered the secret of extremely long life – 800 or 900 years – and some of the party tried to take this secret by force. The party was expelled from the valley, which is how we know about its existence.

When the Greek gods divided the Cosmos between them, Poseidon, the Lord of the Ocean, was given Atlantis. Poseidon explored it and found a beautiful woman called Cleito living there. He and Cleito had ten sons, and each ruled over over one tenth of the kingdom. Atlas, the firstborn, became king of the central island. All the people who live on Atlantis are descended from the brothers.

The city of Atlantis flourished and grew rich, for there was copper, timber and many fruits on the island. The houses were built of red, black and white marble and the roofs were of red copper that shone in the sun. On the central island there were two temples. One, dedicated to Poseidon and Cleito, was surrounded by a golden wall. The other, dedicated to Poseidon alone, had silver walls, golden pinnacles and a roof of ivory, gold, silver and copper.

Atlantean scientists discovered many secrets of the universe, but they explored too far. They released the fiery powers of the earth which broke Atlantis apart. Her ruins lie under the Atlantic Ocean.

CENTRE EARTH

O n 26 June each year at noon, it is said that the tip of the shadow of Mount Scartaris in Iceland points the way to the centre of the earth. In the crater of the extinct volcano Sneffels Yokul is a deep chimney

that leads down to a gigantic cavern. Professor Otto Lidenbrock and his nephew Axel are supposed to have gone there in 1863.

The two men found a deep sea enveloped in clouds of mist that illuminated the cavern with a cold white light. Beaches of fine yellow sand were strewn with shells and the bones of prehistoric animals. Along the northern shore were forests of enormous mushrooms. To the south were horsetails and tree ferns, brown and faded because they were deprived of sunlight.

Many huge creatures from prehistoric times still survive at Centre Earth. In the sea Professor Lidenbrock saw a plesiosaurus fight with an ichthyosaurus, and herds of mastodon browsed in the forests. There was even a creature that looked like a giant human.

Professor Lidenbrock built a raft of fossilized wood and navigated past geysers, water spouts and stretches of boiling water. He struggled through electrical storms and fierce gales. Eventually he blasted a tunnel through the southern end of the cavern and ended up in the bowels of a live volcano, which shot the raft and its occupants back up to the surface.

FOUNTAIN OF YOUTH

M any men have searched in vain for the secret of Eternal Youth. One such was Juan Ponce de Leon, who sailed with Christopher Columbus on his second voyage to the West Indies. Ponce de Leon became governor of

Puerto Rico, and it was there that he heard about a magic spring on an island called Bimini. According to the local people, anyone who bathed in the spring would be cured of any ailment and become young and strong again.

Ponce de Leon was an elderly man, weakened by tropical fevers. He was so eager to find the Fountain of Youth that he set off on a new voyage in search of the wonderful island.

In April 1513, on the day known to the Spaniards as Pascua Florida, the Feast of the Flowers, Ponce de Leon discovered a new land and called it Florida. He explored this new land, but could not find the Fountain of Youth and set out again in search of Bimini. But he never found the magic spring, even though he searched all the surrounding islands.

People still look for the Fountain of Youth, but the island of Bimini seems to lie where it has always been, just over the horizon.

HYPERBOREA

The ancient Greeks believed that the earth was flat and circular, with their own country occupying the middle of it. The central point was either Mount Olympus, the abode of the gods, or Delphi, famous for its oracle. The circular disc of the earth was divided into two equal parts by the Sea.

The northern portion of the earth was inhabited by a happy race of people called the Hyperboreans. Their land was almost inaccessible by land or sea, so no other race was able to wage war on them. They were also free of disease, so all the Hyperboreans lived to be at least a thousand years old.

Visitors to Hyperborea could only come during the summer, when there was six months of perpetual sunshine. The winters, when the sun never rose, also lasted six months. The Hyperboreans spent the winters asleep in comfortable caves. They only came out when the sun rose again.

◁ Hyperborea had very unusual plant life and animals. In the forests tree trunks grew into the shape of human beings. Unicorns lived there too, and a multitude of colourful birds. The strangest animals of all were the two-headed frogs, which the Hyperboreans liked to eat for their dinner.

Magical Creatures

Several different kinds of magical creatures are mentioned in the old legends. Often they are humans who have been put under a spell, which needs to be broken before they can return to their natural state. Some creatures are fairies in animal or tree form, with special magical powers. Others are the pets, or familiars, of witches and wizards; or fairy domestic animals, which are different from human cattle and horses and often of a superior breed.

The White Cat

There was once an aged king who had three grown-up sons. One day he called the princes to him and said, 'The time has come for me to give up the throne and retire to the country. I would like to have a dog to keep me company. Whichever one of you brings me the smallest and prettiest dog will inherit the crown. Go now and return in one year.'

The three brothers set out in different directions. The youngest prince took a road that led through the forest, but just as he reached the middle of it there was a dreadful thunderstorm. Rain fell in torrents and soaked him to the skin. Worst of all, he lost his way in the darkness. The prince wandered about for several hours until suddenly he saw a bright light shimmering through the trees. Hastening towards it, he found himself at the entrance to a magnificent castle made of solid gold studded with diamonds.

The prince pulled the bell chain and the gate opened. No one was there, but invisible hands urged him inside and guided him through endless suites of magnificently furnished rooms. Then the hands settled him down in a comfortable armchair in front of a fire. His wet clothes were removed and replaced with a suit of the finest materials.

A sumptuous banquet appeared and, as the prince was about to eat, a white cat entered the room and sat on a golden stool. She wore a coronet

and a silver veil, and was the daintiest little animal the prince had ever seen. Then she asked him who he was and how he came to her castle.

The cat listened to his story, and then invited him to enjoy the meal. As soon as he drank wine from the crystal goblet, the prince forgot all about his quest – he stayed with the white cat in her castle. During the day they went riding, the prince on a wooden horse and the cat on a monkey. In the evenings the cat sang to him, in the sweetest voice he had ever heard.

It was almost a year since the prince left home when the cat said to him, 'You have only three days left to look for the little dog your father asked for.'

The prince was dismayed that he had forgotten his quest, but the cat came to his rescue and gave him an acorn. When he opened it at his father's court he found that it contained the tiniest dog in the world, so small it could jump through a lady's ring.

The king was speechless with wonder. There was no doubt as to which son had brought the prettiest and smallest dog. But the king didn't want to give up the crown quite yet, so he told his sons that he would give them another year to find a piece of linen so fine it would pass through the eye of a needle.

The prince went straight back to the white cat's castle and stayed there for another year. When it was time to go back to the court the cat gave him a walnut. The two older brothers had brought exquisite linen, and the king laughed when the youngest produced a walnut and cracked it.

Inside the walnut was a hazelnut; and inside that a cherry stone. The prince cracked the cherry stone and took out the kernel. Inside the kernel he found a grain of wheat, and in the wheat one grain of bird seed. He opened the seed, and to the amazement of all the court, drew out a piece of linen four hundred yards long, painted with the moon and stars and all kinds of birds and animals. The linen passed easily through the eye of the tiniest needle.

The youngest brother had clearly won both contests, but still the king was not ready to retire.

'Travel for another year,' he said to his sons, 'and the one who brings home the most beautiful princess shall marry her and be crowned king.'

Again the prince returned to the white cat's castle, and so another year passed until it was almost time for him to return to court with a prospective bride. Instead of producing a magic gift as she had done before, this time the cat asked the prince to cut off her head and tail and throw them into the fire.

The prince was horrified and for several days refused to do as she asked. But at last she persuaded him that both his own happiness and hers depended on his complying with her request. Then, with trembling hand, he drew his sword and cut off both her head and tail. Instantly the cat changed into the most beautiful girl he had ever seen. The girl told the prince that his action had broken the spell that she was under.

'I have not always been a cat,' she said. 'My father was the monarch of six kingdoms. My mother, the Queen, wanted to taste forbidden fruits that grew in an enchanted garden. In return for the fruits she had to promise to hand over her baby daughter to the fairies. As soon as I was born the fairies came to claim me. They brought me up very well and built a tower for me to live in.

'One day I looked out of the window and saw a handsome young knight with whom I fell in love. However, the fairies wanted me to marry an ugly dwarf. When I refused they turned me into a white cat and brought me to this palace. They changed all the lords and ladies of my father's kingdom into cats, too, and made them invisible.

'The fairies told me that I would remain a cat until I found another prince to rescue me. You, my love, have done just that, and now all my troubles are over.'

White Cat, now a princess, climbed into a magnificent chariot and with the prince at her side set out for his father's palace. By the time they arrived the two older brothers were already walking in the palace grounds with two beautiful princesses. White Cat hid herself in a piece of rock crystal.

The king looked at his youngest son and said, 'So you come alone this time?'

'Father,' replied the prince, handing him the piece of crystal, 'inside this you will find a little white cat that mews so sweetly I am sure it will please you.'

As he spoke the crystal fell apart and the princess stepped out, like the sun appearing from behind clouds, her golden hair hanging in long curls to her feet.

'This is the one who has won the crown,' the king exclaimed.

'Sire,' said the princess, 'I do not wish to deprive you of your throne. I have six kingdoms of my own. Please allow me to give one to each of your two elder sons, and in exchange I ask for the hand of your youngest son as my husband.'

So the marriages of all three brothers were celebrated together, and then the three couples set off, each to govern their own kingdom.

TALKING TREES

Many countries have folk-tales about trees that talk. In Sherwood Forest in England there is a huge elm that hunters often ask for advice about where to find their prey. In Ireland the trees are particularly talkative and will offer advice to anyone who is looking for treasure hidden by leprechauns.

One man was saved from starvation by a friendly tree. He was shipwrecked on the island of Tonga in the Pacific Ocean and had nothing to eat. A puko tree told him to break off one of its branches and bake it in an earth oven. The branch turned into a meal of yams and pork and the man was saved.

UNICORNS

Unicorns were once thought to be common in the countries of the northern hemisphere. They roamed the forests of China, Japan, Arabia, India and North Africa, as well as Europe. Unicorn means 'one-horn', and they were given this name because of the single horn in the middle of their forehead. Otherwise they have the head and body of a horse, the legs of an antelope, the tail of a lion and the beard of a goat.

Unicorns are solitary animals and do not move around together in herds. The unicorn's horn is a fearsome weapon and the male unicorn is very savage, protecting his territory fiercely. Foals are born without a horn, and stay with their mothers until the horn has grown to its full length before going off on their own.

Drinking from a unicorn horn cup protects you against poisoned wine, and crushed horn is said to be a cure for all kinds of disease. But unicorns move so fast that it is impossible to catch them. The only way to trap one is to stand in front of a large tree and let it charge, then jump aside at the last moment so that it drives its horn into the tree.

◁◁ The stories say that it is difficult to describe the voice of a tree. They say it is like a combination of murmuring, sighing, rustling and creaking. You should always be careful if you hear a tree speak clearly to you. It might be a spirit and they are not necessarily friendly to mortals.

△ Japanese legends tell of a creature like a unicorn, called a *baiku*, which eats bad dreams. It wanders around at night, eating the dreams as they are dispatched by ghosts and other unfriendly spirits.

PEGASUS

Pegasus was a magnificent white stallion with golden wings. According to one of the Greek legends, when the hero Perseus cut off the head of Medusa, Pegasus sprang from her body.

A young warrior called Bellerophon tamed the horse with a bridle given to him by the goddess Athena. He then mounted Pegasus and flew off in search of adventure.

Bellerophon slew the fire-breathing dragon Chimera and overcame the Amazons, but then he grew ambitious and tried to fly to heaven. Zeus, the king of the gods, was angry at Bellerophon's boldness and sent an insect to tickle Pegasus and make him throw his rider. Pegasus went on flying up to heaven and was changed into a group of stars. On a starlit night you can still see him there today.

ELEPHANTS' GRAVEYARD

When old elephants know that the time has come to leave this world, they plod off to a secret valley in the jungle where they lay down and die. For centuries men have sought these elephant graveyards, hoping to make their fortune from the ivory of their tusks.

In one of the tales of *The Arabian Nights*, Sinbad the Sailor shoots elephants for his master, until one day a huge elephant tears up the tree in which he is hiding and carries him to a field covered with the tusks of dead elephants. The elephant knew that it was only their tusks that Sinbad wanted, and took him to their burying place, so that he could get all he wanted without killing them.

CATS

Cats have always been associated with magic and mystery. Witches can see into the future by means of animal familiars, and these are often cats.

In Ireland in particular, fairies often take the form of a cat. They are usually evil, but there is one story of an amiable fairy cat.

An old woman was sitting up late spinning in her cottage, when there was a knock at the door and a black cat walked in, followed by two white kittens, and sat down by the fire.

The old woman said not a word, but continued spinning while the cats washed themselves in front of the fire. After a while the black cat told the old woman to stop spinning and go to bed because she was stopping the fairies from enjoying their nightly revels.

'If it were not for me and my daughters,' said the cat, 'you would be dead by now. Give us a drink of milk and we'll be off, and mind you don't sit up late again.'

So the old woman fetched a bowl of milk, and the cats lapped it up and shot off up the chimney. After they had gone she found a silver coin in the ashes – enough to pay for many nights' spinning. After that the old woman followed the cat's advice and never sat up late again.

△ Cats were worshipped in ancient Egypt. The goddess Bast had a cat's head – she looked after the crops and made sure that children were born with wisdom and beauty.

OWLS

The owl was a bird that was sacred to Athena, the ancient Greek goddess of wisdom. Because of this, owls are always considered to be wise old birds with mystical powers. In many African countries south of the Sahara, the melancholy call of the owl is associated with bad luck.

Owls are active at night, so they are much valued by witches and other magicians, who often keep them as pets, or familiars. Some witches are said to turn themselves into owls, and then they swoop down to peck off the limbs of their victims.

Magical Implements

Traditionally, certain materials and objects bring a person good luck and protect them from evil spirits. The most powerful of these is iron, which is why it is said to be lucky to have a horseshoe on or over your front door. Amber is also considered lucky. Both iron and amber are used to ward off black magic.

Even today people wear lucky charms against failing exams or losing a football match. In myths and legends from all around the world, people are helped in their tasks by an implement given to them by the gods or the fairies.

NAILS

Nails have magical qualities and if you lay one on top of your belongings it is supposed to stop the fairies from spiriting them away. If you carry one in your pocket, it will stop you being led astray by pixies. Iron nails driven into the door in the shape of a cross will stop evil spirits from entering a house. Water spirits can be pinned down by soaking nails in the river and hammering them into a tree.

AMULET

An amulet is a charm which protects a person from evil spirits or witchcraft. Depending on the beliefs of its

wearer, it might be in the shape of a cross, or perhaps a Buddha. Some amulets contain herbs to guard against illness.

Amulets can also protect people from danger. The men of Sulawesi used to wear a piece of coral on a string round their necks to make them invulnerable in battle. Other warriors wore a phial of sacred oil or tiger teeth.

Sometimes an amulet is used to deter thieves. In Indonesia animal figures with red eyes were hung in fruit trees, and these will wound a thief if he touches the fruit.

RINGS

Rings are supposed to have special powers because the essential force of the metal cannot escape from the unbroken circle. They are most often made to fit fingers, but may also be worn as bracelets or coronets. Seamen have always worn rings in their ears because they strengthen eyesight. The ring Draupnir, made by the dwarves for the god Odin, could increase its owner's wealth. The Ring of the Nibelungen had similar powers.

BELLS

Fairies cannot tolerate the sound of bells. If you fear that an evil spirit has taken up residence in your home, the tinkling of a bell will drive it away.

It was church bells that drove the trolls away from Denmark. A young couple were visited one night by a tiny man with a hunchback and a long white beard. The troll had come as an

▽▽ Stone circles are said to be focuses of mystic power and to be built at the point where lines of earth power, called 'ley lines', cross. Stonehenge on Salisbury Plain in England is one of the most famous stone circles in the world, but there are hundreds of others across Europe.

ambassador from his king, who lived in a hill nearby and was anxious that his subjects should not be molested by humans. The young couple and the trolls became good neighbours, helping each other out in emergencies.

Then one day the couple were invited to a farewell banquet, and the king told them that the trolls could no longer stay in Denmark because they were so many church bells everywhere. They were forced to migrate to the wilder, lonelier countryside of Norway.

CLAY

Many peoples believe that clay was the material from which mankind and the other creatures on earth were originally created. The Creation Ancestor moulded a male and female figure out of clay and added pebbles for eyes and dried grass for hair. The clay figures were left in the sun to dry, and then the Creator blew the breath of life into them.

The Creator took much more trouble with animals than he did with humans. Because of this, each animal looks almost exactly the same as all the others of its species – whereas every human looks different and the clay figures range all the way from ugly to beautiful.

In Africa the people say that God created people from different types of earth. He took white loam for the white man, brownish earth for the Arabs, but for the black people he used the best earth – the fertile black clay from the banks of the River Nile. Some Africans still

▽ Many sculptors and wood carvers say that their greatest creations come from inside the clay or the wood. 'All I had to do was to set it free – it was inside already....'

maintain that God creates good people out of good clay and bad people out of stinking mud.

CORN DOLLY

C orn is the staple food for many peoples of the world and is therefore regarded as the symbol of life and fertility. A spirit exists in every grain field, and must be placated to ensure a good harvest. At harvest time the last sheaf from each field is made into a Corn Dolly, in which the spirit lives until the following year. When seeds are planted in the spring, the Corn Dolly is buried in the ground so that the spirit is released. If this is not done and the spirit is trapped, the new crop will be poor.

Corn Dollies are sometimes known as Kern Babies, or in Scotland as Maidens or Carlins. Elsewhere in Europe they have a variety of different names such as Corn Mother, Corn Maiden, Corn Wolf or Oats Stallion.

Originally Corn Dollies were made simply by tying a bundle of grain so that it looked as if it had a head and a body, like a doll. But country craftspeople soon found ways of weaving the dry stalks and ears of corn into wreaths and other elaborate designs.

RUNES

R unes were the earliest form of writing used by the Scandinavian people. They were often used for magic purposes. In Sweden a stone was

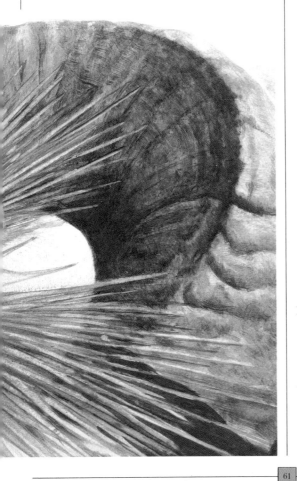

found that had on it this inscription: 'This is the secret meaning on the runes. I hid here power-runes, undisturbed by evil witchcraft. He who destroys this monument shall die in exile by means of magic art.' Other rune inscriptions were used to ward off witches.

◁ It is said that Odin, the one-eyed god of the Vikings, won the first runes from the Norns. He found the Norns spinning the lifelines of mortals under Yggdrasil (see page 68) and gave one of his eyes in exchange for the secret of the runes.

MASKS

▽ These six masks come from as far afield as ancient Greece, Nigeria, Northwest Canada and the islands of the Pacific.

Masks are worn by witch doctors to chase away evil spirits. Or sometimes a person who puts on a mask can by some mysterious power become the evil spirit or animal he is imitating.

Masks are often used in religious rituals and other ceremonies. Their function is to express the people's hopes and fears, to revive their ancestors, or to strengthen bonds with friendly spirits. In Mali the men celebrate the god of the waters, Faro, who created fishes in the River Niger. Every year a new mask is carved for the god. It might have human or animal features, or a

combination of both. A mask has big eyes, nostrils and ears in order to see, smell and hear people's bad deeds. The square chin represents purity and firmness of decision.

Masks may also be used to cure illness. In some countries it is thought that if someone is ill their soul has been stolen by the dead. The medicine man puts on a magic mask and goes to the graveyard in search of the lost soul, the mask giving him the power to seize back the soul from the dead.

KNOTS

Many people think that tying a knot creates magical powers. A knot in your handkerchief will remind you of something that you should do. Knots should be used carefully though, because they can cause trouble. If a group of people at a meeting find that they cannot agree, then one of them probably has a knot somewhere on their person. Untying a knot usually results in the unknotting of an argument.

In the days of sailing ships a captain would make sure he had a magical knotted cord before embarking on a voyage. There were three knots in the cord which could be untied to release a wind if his ship was becalmed. The first knot released a moderate breeze, the second a strong wind, and the third a gale.

Probably the most famous knot, known as the Gordian Knot, was in a temple in the town of Gordium in Asia Minor. The story was that only the man who was going to conquer Asia would be able to undo it. Alexander the Great did not even try to untie it – he simply drew his sword and cut the knot with one blow. Then he led his army of Greeks and Macedonians from Greece to the plains of India, winning every battle as he went.

SWORDS

Legendary heroes often had magic swords that gave them extraordinary powers over their enemies. The Irish hero Cu Chulainn did battle with human enemies, supernatural beings and monsters armed with the sword Caladbolg. Roland, the French warrior who defeated a vast army of Saracens at Roncesvalles almost single-handed, fought with the sword Durendal.

The swords wielded by the heroes always came into their possession by magical means. The great sword of Sigmund Volsung was thrust through a tree trunk by the god Odin, and Sigmund was the only warrior strong enough to

wrench it out again. Similarly, in medieval England, fifteen year-old Arthur became king by pulling a sword from a stone when all the knights had failed to do so. Later his magic sword Excalibur was given to him by a hand that appeared out of the lake at Avalon.

Often a magic sword is only effective if wielded by a courageous hero. When it is used by an ordinary man its blade becomes blunt and ineffective. The sword of the Albanian hero Iskander Beg is a good example.

Magic swords are also familiar in Japanese and Chinese legends. The Japanese hero Yamato had a sacred sword called Cloud Cluster, which had been taken from the tail of the Great Serpent. When he left it behind with his loved one as a memento, he was no longer protected by its power and so was killed by a monster.

In China it is said that the clefts in the Great Dyke of Stone, the Annamite Chain, were made by magic swords. A slave named Fan Wen found two carp in a mountain stream that changed themselves first into whetstones for sharpening tools, and then into iron ore.

Fan Wen smelted the ore and forged two swords. Then he raised the blades towards the Great Dyke and uttered a prayer. 'The carp transformed themselves into stone; the swords have been made from the smelting of the iron. If they indeed have magic power, let the stone be cleft, let the Dyke be broken. If this be achieved, I shall become the ruler of the realm.' Fan Wen later became one of the greatest emperors of China.

Seeing the Unknown

Most people want to know what is going to happen to them in the future. We have our fortunes told for fun, but in some parts of the world fortune-telling is taken very seriously. The idea that signs or omens could foretell future happenings is very old. To ancient peoples the things that happened in the heavens were the most important of all, and they believed that by studying the positions of the stars in the skies they could forecast the fate and future of human beings.

ORACLES

An oracle is a place where people consult the gods about the future or about the meaning of things that have happened to them. The gods speak through a medium, who is usually a woman, although sometimes it may be an animal or a natural feature such as a tree.

People who consult oracles believe that events are caused by gods, spirits or witches. If they are suddenly sick, or when a disaster happens, they consult an oracle to discover the reason, thinking that their own bad or careless behaviour may have angered the gods or spirits. The oracle then tells them how to make amends.

One of the most famous oracles was the Talking Oak of Dodona, a huge tree that stood in the middle of a forest. A person who wanted to consult the oracle shouted his query up into the branches

◁◁ Apollo, the Greek god of music and prophecy, and Athena, the goddess of wisdom, were the main patrons of oracles. Athena was known to deliver her own oracles, disguised as a bird of prey.

and the Tree replied by rustling its leaves. Priests then interpreted the answer.

The best-known oracle of ancient Greece was at Delphi on Mount Parnassus. Apollo, Greek god of the sun, spoke through a priestess called the Pythia. When asked a question, the priestess chewed a leaf of the laurel, Apollo's sacred plant, and drank the waters of an underground stream. Then she sat on a golden tripod in the centre of the temple and breathed in vapour that rose from a crack in the floor.

As the spirit took possession of her body, the Pythia writhed and muttered strange sounds. Priests wrote down the meaning of her words, usually in verse, and these were handed to the questioner as the reply of the oracle. Often the answers given by the oracle were not clear and could be understood in two different ways. This made it difficult to prove that the oracle was wrong.

THE SIGNS OF THE ZODIAC

The first sign of the zodiac, close to the planet Mars, is Aries the Ram. Aries was once the leader of a flock owned by the god Mars. Aries causes plants and animals to reproduce in the spring.

Taurus the Bull, the second sign, is stubborn, but loyal and extremely protective towards the cows and calves in his herd.

Gemini is the name for the twin sons of Zeus, Castor and Pollux. They were lively, adventurous young men, always looking for excitement. Anyone born between May and June, when the house of Gemini is in the ascendant, is likely to be the same.

Cancer, like all crabs, is retiring by nature. Cancer was a sentry for the nine-headed monster Hydra. Hercules crushed Cancer, but she

▷ The ancient Babylonians who lived in what is now Iraq, were the first to chart the houses of the Zodiac more than 5,000 years ago. The zodiacal year starts in March because that was the month when the Babylonian New Year was celebrated.

was rescued by the goddess Hera and placed in the heavens as a symbol of the Great Mother.

Leo the Lion is a powerful sign because he is related to both the sun and the moon. This magnificent creature reigns over the summer months of July and August and has always been a symbol of courage, nobility and enterprise. Leo is a born leader of men, confident and assured – but sometimes people born under this sign can be just a little too vain and dictatorial.

Virgo, the sixth sign, was the daughter of King Icarius. When her father was killed by shepherds she hanged herself from a tree. It was the time of year when all the crops were ripening, but not yet harvested, so Virgo became the symbol of ripening womanhood.

Libra, the Golden Scales, has a dual personality. Sometimes she is under the control of Venus, a symbol of peace and happiness. At other times she tips the scales in favour of Aphrodite and becomes wild and unruly.

Scorpio, like the insect which is her symbol, does not harm those who leave her alone, but for those who cross her, her sting is deadly. Scorpio is descended from Selket, the Scorpion-goddess of Egypt.

Sagittarius the Archer was once a centaur called Cheiron. As a centaur he was a wise ruler and trained many of the famous Greek heroes. When Cheiron was wounded by a poisoned arrow, Zeus rewarded him for his services by changing him into a constellation.

Capricorn is the constellation of the great god Pan. He has the body

and arms of a man, but the hindquarters of a goat. Pan's favourite occupation was chasing nymphs through the woods and causing trouble, and people born under the sign of Capricorn often have the same habits.

Aquarius was the cupbearer of the Gods until Zeus rewarded him with immortality and place him in the heavens as a constellation.

Pisces swims through the watery regions of the twelfth house of the Zodiac, flooding the northern hemisphere with rain to ensure good crops in the summer.

AUGUR

An augur is a person who interprets omens and signs from the gods. In order to do this, the augur must sit on top of a high hill on a cloudless night. He sits inside a sacred circle,

called a templum, which he has consecrated by offering prayers to Jupiter, the Roman god of thunder. Any sign that comes from the east is favourable; those from the west are unfavourable. For example, a flash of lightning to the east is an indication of Jupiter's favour.

Other omens might include thunder claps, falling stars or birds. The most significant birds are eagles, vultures, owls, crows and ravens. Several eagles flying from east to west would be extremely auspicious (showing good fortune).

YGGDRASIL

According to Norse legend, the world was shaped from the body of a huge giant. The arch of heaven was his skull, which rested on the shoulders of four strong dwarfs at the world's corners. The Earth, called Midgard, was supported by the great ash tree Yggdrasil. The tree had three large roots: one extended into Asgard, the home of the Gods; another into the land of the Frost Giants; and the third into the Kingdom of the Dead.

The tree was watered by a well tended by the Norns, who were three weird sisters. Urd (Fate) could see everything that had happened in the past. Verlandi (Being) had the power of knowing what was going on everywhere in the world at the present time. Skuld (Necessity), the wisest of all, could see into the future, which even Odin himself could not do.

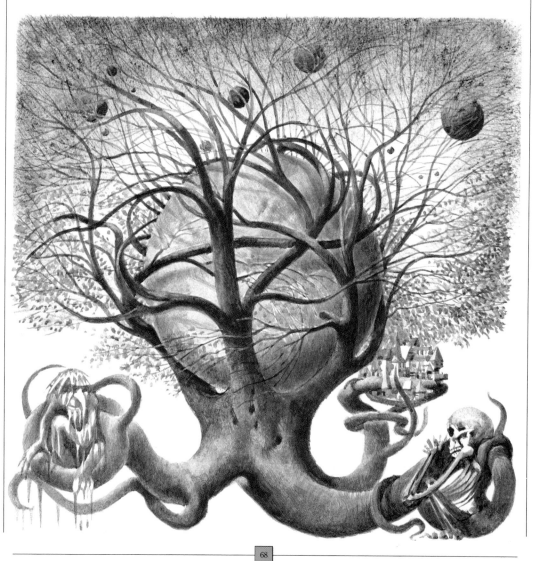

▷ Yggdrasil was called the Tree of the World and sometimes the Tree of Life in Norse mythology. It was tended by the Norns, who also spun the thread of each mortal's life and cut it short at the decreed moment.

The Norns often appeared at the birth of a hero to determine his fate and give him gifts of good and evil. They told Odin what was going to happen in the world, and from them he learned about the Last Battle – which must come when the Gods and their giant foes fight a final contest between Good and Evil and the world would end.

CRYSTALS

People have used all sorts of different things for looking into the future, ranging from water in a coconut shell or ink in a glass bowl to glass or metal mirrors, but there is no doubt that crystal is the most effective.

The ideal shape is that of a ball, and the crystal should be clear, otherwise the future will be partially obscured. A professional crystal-gazer can see things happening in a crystal ball as clearly as an ordinary person can see things on television.

Crystals have a place in the mythology of many countries. Among the Hopi people of North America, a medicine man diagnosed what was wrong with a sick person by laying his hands on their body. If the illness was caused by bad thoughts sent by another person, the medicine man would take a small crystal from his pouch and hold it up to the sun to awaken it. He would then look through the crystal to see the face of the person causing the trouble.

ALECTROMANCY

This is a way of foretelling the future using a cockerel and grains of corn. Tether the cockerel to a stake with a piece of cord, and then draw a circle in the dust around it. Write the letters of the alphabet round the outside of the circle and put a grain of corn on each letter. Now put your question to the cockerel and watch which letters he pecks the corn from. Replace the grains in case he needs to use the same letter more than once. When the cockerel has finished, the letters he has pecked from should spell out your answer.

Witches

itch is the name given to someone who is believed to be in league with the devil and to possess evil and magical powers. All over the world people have believed in witches. In Europe witches were supposed to be able to fly through the air on broomsticks, wearing pointed black hats and with a cat for company. Today, in parts of Mexico and Africa, witches and witch-doctors still have great power in their tribes.

▷ Three famous witches from Scotland were the coven whom Macbeth, the Thane of Cawdor, met after a great battle. They prophesied correctly that he would become Thane of Glamis and King of Scotland, but the prophecy also led him to murder and to an inglorious death.

Witches are usually female, and there are two types. Black witches possess evil powers and are in league with the devil. They cast spells with the help of demons and other corrupt spirits. White witches get their magical power from saints and angels and work for the good of the community, for example preparing medicines from herbs. Male witches are called warlocks.

All witches can bewitch people, cast spells and turn themselves into animals. They can also see into the future by means of animals which are called familiars. Often these animals are cats, but they could also be dogs, ravens or toads. White witches usually communicate with the other world by crystal gazing and other similarly harmless pursuits.

White witches gain their knowledge from a close study of nature and by reading herbals (books of lore about herbs and natural remedies). Black witchcraft is taught only by word of mouth. Witches are interested in knowledge for its own sake, regardless of whether or not they are having an effect on humans.

Accomplished black witches pass on their craft by taking on students. Anyone wanting to become a pupil

has to go through an initiation ceremony standing naked in front of witnesses. She places her right hand on her head, then raises her right foot and places her left hand on her heel. She must then vow to surrender to Satan, Lord of Hell, all that lies between her hands.

The novice witch then becomes an associate member of a coven of thirteen witches, but cannot be a full member until one of the other witches has been exorcised, taken by the Devil, burnt at the stake, or robbed of her powers in some other way.

In the Dark Ages in Europe, before the spread of Christianity, most people worshipped pagan gods. Religious ceremonies were held at great tombs of stone, some of which can still be seen and are known as dolmens or cromlechs. There are many of them in parts of Spain, Portugal, France, Cornwall, Ireland and Denmark.

In time these monuments were looked on not only as tombs of dead leaders, but as places from which spirits of the dead could come to be born again in new people. These old stone monuments were therefore often the centres where witches gathered.

The god whom the witches worshipped was often in the form of

▷ A novice black witch takes her oath to Satan. By doing this, she is condemning her soul to everlasting suffering after her death. Only the most wicked or desperate witches do this; most witches are white.

an animal with horns – a stag, bull or goat. People depended for their living on their crops, and so the four largest ceremonies of worship, known as Sabbats, were connected with the change of seasons through the year. The first was Candlemas in February, then Walpurgis night or May Eve, Lammas in August and Hallowe'en on 31 October.

Hallowe'en is the eve of All Saints Day when Christians remember the dead. Then the spirits of the dead visit their living relations for comfort. There are all kinds of occult happenings going on. Flocks of witches fly to the final Sabbat of the year – but you can frighten them away with a bonfire.

Besides the Sabbats, witches used to meet at night in groups of thirteen called covens. Often their meetings were held on Fridays, which is why Friday the 13th is considered to be an unlucky day.

After Christianity came, the Church hunted down anyone who still worshipped pagan gods as a witch and put them to death, usually by drowning or burning them.

▽ Witches must make their own besom, or riding broom, in the traditional way from willow twigs. These must be firmly bound to a strong handle; then the broom is enchanted using the correct spells. Witches prefer the old-fashioned broom because it provides a passenger seat for their familiar.

Baba Yaga

In Russian folk tales a great part is played by the Baba Yaga, the old thunder witch. She lives in a miserable little hut in the forest propped up on hen's legs, and flies through the air at dawn and twilight pursuing a course of cruel destruction. In this story Baba Yaga is jealous of an old princess and her attractive son and daughter, and thinks up an evil plot to destroy them.

One day Baba Yaga paid a visit to the old princess and said, 'My dear friend, put this ring on your son's finger and he will always be healthy and rich. But he must not take the ring off until he finds the maiden that it fits. She is the one he must marry.'

The princess believed Baba Yaga and just before she died she reminded her son, Prince Danila Govorila, that he must find a wife on whose finger the ring would fit. The prince travelled far and wide in search of a bride. He tried the ring on all the eligible young maidens, but found that it was either too big or too small. Eventually he returned home in despair.

His sister Catherine asked why he was looking so pensive and sad. When he told her what the trouble was, she said, 'I can't believe that ring is such a problem. Let me try it.'

The magic ring clasped the princess's finger and gleamed brightly. It fitted as though it had been made for her.

'Dear sister,' said Prince Danila Govorila, 'fate has chosen you for my wife.'

'What are you saying?' cried the princess. 'You cannot marry your own sister! It is against every law there is.'

The prince took no notice of her and ordered that preparations be made immediately for the wedding. The princess rushed out of the palace into the garden. She was sitting by the fountain weeping when some old women passed by.

'Don't cry,' they said, 'just do as we say and everything will be all right. Make four little dolls, and put them in the four corners of your room. Go to your wedding, but when your brother calls you to the bridal chamber, do not hurry.'

So the brother married his sister, and in due course called her to his chamber. 'I will come in a minute,' she replied. 'I am taking off my earrings.'

The dolls in the four corners cried like cuckoos:

Cuckoo, Prince Danila,
Cuckoo, Govorila,
Cuckoo, he takes his sister,
Cuckoo, for a wife,
Cuckoo, earth open wide,
Cuckoo, sister, fall inside!

The earth opened and Catherine began to fall inside.

Her brother called to her again and she said, 'Just a minute, let me undo my girdle.'

The dolls cuckooed, and Catherine fell into the earth a little further so that only her head was still above ground.

Again Prince Danila Govorila called her, and this time she said, 'Wait, brother, while I take off my slippers.'

The dolls cuckooed once more and the princess vanished into the earth. Angry now, the prince ran to Catherine's room to look for her, and when he found only the dolls sitting in the corners he seized an axe and cut off their heads.

The princess walked underground until she came out of the mouth of a cave. There in front of her was a little hut standing on chicken legs. Inside sat a beautiful girl embroidering a tablecloth with silver and gold threads.

'You are welcome to come in, ' she said. 'But there will be trouble for both of us when my mother gets back. She is the witch Baba Yaga.'

They sat at the embroidery frame together and talked, until Vasilissa heard her mother coming. Then she turned Catherine into a needle, stuck it into a birch broom and stood the broom in a corner.

'I smell a Russian bone,' said the witch as soon as she came inside.

'Some passers-by came in for a drink of water,' said the girl. 'They were old people, mother, and would not have been to your liking.'

'Well, next time someone calls by, make sure you invite them into the house and do not let them go,' said the witch.

The witch flew off on her broom and the girls continued with the embroidery until she came back. Again she sniffed about in the house and said, 'I smell a Russian bone.'

'Some little old men came in to warm their hands,' said Vasilissa. 'I tried to keep them, but they did not want to stay.'

The witch was hungry. She scolded her daughter and went out again. The girls quickly finished the embroidery and were planning how to escape from the wicked witch when the princess noticed her standing in the doorway. Her heart missed a beat: before her stood Baba Yaga the Bony-legged, her long nose hitting the ceiling.

'Daughter,' said the witch happily, 'stoke up the fire so that I can cook our supper.'

When the fire was blazing the witch took a shovel and told Catherine to sit on it. She pushed her towards the mouth of the stove, but the princess put one leg into the stove and the other on top of it.

'You don't know how to sit girl,' said the witch crossly. 'Sit the right way.'

The princess changed her posture, but this time she put one leg into the stove and the other under it. The witch grew really angry and pulled her out again. 'You are playing tricks, young woman,' she said. 'Look, I will show you how to do it.'

Baba Yaga sat down on the shovel and stretched out her legs. Quick as a flash, the two girls shoved her into the stove and locked her in. Then they picked up the embroidery and a brush and comb and ran.

Looking back, they saw the witch, who had wrenched the oven door off, coming after them. They threw down the brush and a thick marsh overgrown with reeds appeared behind them. The witch could not crawl through it, but she plucked out a path with her claws.

Then the girls threw down the comb, and a thick forest appeared behind them. The witch sharpened her teeth and bit off the trees, one by one, at their roots.

The girls ran and ran until they could run no longer. Finally they threw down the embroidered tablecloth, and a sea of fire spread behind them. Baba Yaga flew high across the sea, but the bindings of her broom burned through. She fell down and was consumed in the flames.

The girls sat down to rest. Just then, Prince Danila Govorila came along and invited them to his home. He knew that one of them was his sister, but both were so beautiful he couldn't be sure which was which.

'I know how we can find out, master,' said the prince's servant. 'Fill a sheep's bladder with blood and put it under your arm. While you are talking to the young ladies I will strike you with a knife in your side. The blood will flow and your sister will reveal herself.'

As soon as Catherine saw the blood she rushed to help her brother. He embraced his sister, and in due course married her to a good man. He himself married Vasilissa, on whose finger the ring fitted. And all of them lived happily ever after.

AFRICAN WITCHES

I n Africa, there are two types of witchcraft. An old woman may be regarded as a witch because her presence makes a child ill. She will be accused of casting the evil eye on the child, perhaps because she is jealous, not having children of her own. In East Africa, the kisirani is a person who by his or her mere presence causes misfortunes, such as precious earthenware falling to pieces as they enter a room. This type of witchcraft is simply a disastrous influence, or the result of being born with ill luck.

Real witches seem to be more vicious in Africa than in other parts of the world. They 'eat' people by devouring the spiritual strength, the life-force, of their victims, so that

they die. Another common form of witchcraft is brewing poison, and secretly putting it in the intended victim's food. The victim will die and his spirit becomes a slave. Like witches from other parts of the world, African ones can change themselves and others into animals. They are said to ride on hyenas to their dances.

◁ African witch doctors (see page 78) are not the same as witches. He or she is more like a white witch, curing illnesses and encouraging the rains to fall. They often use rattles to alert the spirits that something is wanted of them or that their presence has been detected and they must leave the sick person.

Night-witches are invisible in daytime, but can be seen flying at night with fire coming out of their behinds. Anyone who is out in the night will be regarded as a witch, so a warlock will leave an object, such as a broom, or a part of his body behind to answer for him if someone in the hut calls his name.

In their meetings, warlocks share in a communal meal at which they eat the life-energy of their victims. The victim will not even be present, yet after a short time he or she will show signs of illness, and soon will wither away and die without hope. Every member of the coven has to contribute a victim in turn, who will then be consumed at the next convention. Usually the warlock will offer a member of his family.

Many African people believe that witchcraft is hereditary, so there are families of witches. In Zimbabwe, a witch is called to the profession by a dead ancestor who appears as a shadow, or in a dream, or as a cobra. The call must be obeyed.

A sorcerer is believed to be more powerful than a witch. He has an evil spirit who can control other spirits. The sorcerer may make a fetish, a wooden statue or other object, and by his incantations compel a spirit to make its home in it. The statue will then fly like a bird to the selected victim and persecute him. In this way, sorcerers can terrorize whole communities.

WITCH DOCTORS

Witch doctors have much in common with wizards. They make magic to bring rain or a good harvest; or they will perform various rites and ceremonies on sick people to make them better. They are usually the only ones to know spells and rites and are much feared by the rest of the tribe. In cases of sickness, a witch doctor uses a rattle to tell the demon inhabiting a patient's body that it is time to depart.

By his continuous rattling, he keeps the demon awake, so that it must listen to the spells that weaken its powers. Rattles are also used in rain-making ceremonies to enliven the sky spirits; in hunters' dances to imitate the tattoo of animal hooves; in fertility rites to awaken the spirits of creation; in war dances to ask powerful spirits to help the tribe; and in many other tribal ceremonies.

▽ Gagool, who was the chief witch of the Kukuana people, showed Allan Quatermain and his friends the way to the legendary Mine of King Solomon. The mine, which lay somewhere near the borders of modern Angola and Zambia, was guarded by these three colossal statues. Gagool tried to entomb the party in the treasure chamber, but was crushed by the rockfall she had released.

Wizards

Wizards are men who know more than others and who have unusual skills to do the incredible. The abilities of wizards include power over spirits, control of the weather, rapport with the animal kingdom, the capacity to change shape, to fly, to know what is happening far away, to see into the future, to heal the sick and to raise the dead. Like the fairies, wizards can change their shape or that of someone else.

The main occupation of wizards is said to be to cast spells on people. A spell may be a single word ('Abracadabra' is probably the best known), a series of sentences, or sometimes long incantations which can take hours to chant.

Spells are handed down in the wizard community from generation to generation, with instructions to repeat them absolutely correctly. Failure in magic can often be explained by a mistake made in the spell.

An example of the importance of the words used in a spell occurs in the story of Ali Baba in *The Arabian Nights*. Ali Baba's brother could not get out of the thieves' cave because he had forgotten the magic words 'Open Sesame' which made the cave door open.

At the same time as reciting a spell a wizard often has to perform some action, such as a dance or gesture. In rain-making, water is often sprinkled on the ground and drums are beaten to imitate thunder.

Some spells are cast by using pictures made of sand or flower petals. Wizards also have access to secret recipes for magic potions and elixirs. These are often used to make people fall in love.

According to ancient lore, another of the marvels which a competent wizard can make is a door through which you can go and visit your dead parents in the Other World.

Sometimes a wizard is called upon to trap an evil spirit. For this he constructs a cage and sprinkles some human blood under the lever that closes the door. A piece of human flesh is even better. The wizard must then chant an incantation to attract the spirit to the trap. The next morning it should be there, hungry and angry, looking like a wizened child or an old monkey. Sometimes it will look like a big bat, with huge black wings and sharp teeth.

▷ A good wizard is often a friend of the fairies. They would never collaborate with a wizard who practised necromancy or other unpleasant magic. Wizards are often respectable men who hold high positions at court, as Merlin did at the court of King Arthur.

A wizard can also save his friends from ogres by constructing a flying machine. This looks like a basket made of catskin, and it can easily accommodate at least a dozen people. The machine flies just a little faster than the ogres can run, and a little higher than they can jump, but if anyone speaks a word when they are in it they will fall out and be eaten by the ogres.

Wizards are not usually bad, although they are exposed to all the temptations of power and sometimes tend to make use of it. Many necromancers (wizards who raise the dead) start because they want to help someone.

Sometimes people go to an evil wizard when they want to kill an enemy. Then the wizard will make

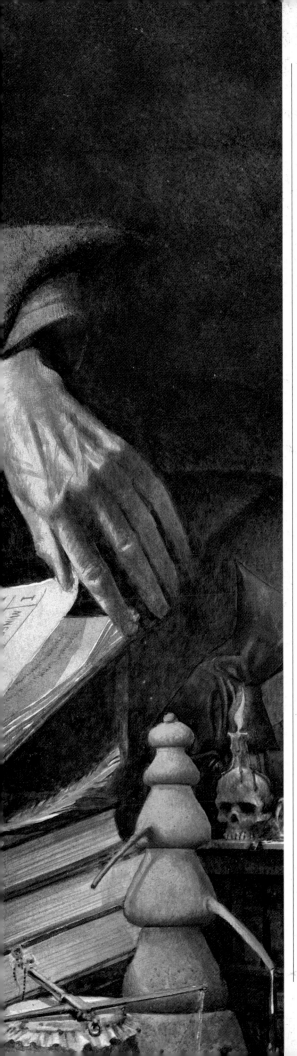

an image in wax or wood and throw it into the fire. If a little of the enemy's hair or skin, or one of his nail cuttings, can be included in the model, the spell is thought to be more powerful. If the person is only to be harmed, the model may be burnt a little in the fire or the wax melted slightly. Sometimes pins may be stuck into it to cause pain.

MERLIN

Merlin, King Arthur's counsellor, was the son of a demon and a virgin. The Arthurian legends tell how the lords of hell plotted to bring about the birth of a devil, but Merlin's mother drank holy water. As a result Merlin had superhuman powers, but did not inherit his father's evil ways.

Merlin was able to change his shape, to create all sorts of illusions and to see into both the past and the future. He first made his mark when Vortigern, King of Britain, was trying to build a castle in the mountains of Wales as a defence against the Saxons. The castle kept falling down, and Merlin divined that there was a pool beneath it where two dragons were fighting – a fact which the court magicians had not been able to discover.

Later, Merlin used his magic art to transport Stonehenge from Ireland to England. He brought about the birth of Arthur and watched over Arthur's early career. It was Merlin who persuaded Arthur's father-in-law, King Urien, to have the Round Table built and Merlin who first revealed the existence of the Holy Grail, the

◁◁ Wizards cannot marry and must spend most of their lives studying. An apprentice must master Latin, Greek, Hebrew, Arabic and at least ten other languages in order to read the standard spell books, which he will have to copy out by hand.

search for which was the greatest adventure of Arthur's knights.

In the end Merlin fell hopelessly in love with an enchantress called Nimue. She persuaded him to tell her the secrets of his magic and then turned his own enchantments against him. Casting a spell of sleep upon him, she chained him up in an oak tree. To this day he remains there, a helpless prisoner.

PROSPERO

I n Shakespeare's play *The Tempest*, Prospero was the Duke of Milan in Italy, but instead of attending to his administrative duties he devoted himself to magic. His younger brother Antonio, helped by the King of Naples, took advantage of this

neglectfulness, and set Prospero and his baby daughter Miranda adrift in a small boat. The boat had no sails, and all they had with them was Prospero's library of books.

The boat drifted on to a small island, and Prospero quickly realized that it was an enchanted place because the air was full of strange music. The island was the home of Ariel and his band of nature sprites. Some time ago the Algerian witch Sycorax and her deformed son, Caliban, had been exiled to the island and tried to convert the nature sprites into evil spirits. When they refused she had imprisoned them all in the trunks of trees.

Prospero used his powers to release Ariel and the other sprites and make them his servants. He found Caliban wandering about the island and took him as a servant.

Some years later a ship carrying Prospero's brother Antonio, the King of Naples and his son Ferdinand passed close to the island. With the help of Ariel and the nature sprites, Prospero created a raging tempest that forced the

△ Prospero was a true wizard, who used books, various pieces of equipment and a staff to work his spells.

ship to take shelter by the shore. He used his magic arts to separate Prince Ferdinand from the others, and Miranda fell in love with him. All the mortals then sailed back to Naples, leaving the island to the freed Ariel and his sprites.

ANGAKUK

An angakuk is an Inuit magician, whose job it is to look after the well-being of his tribe. If bad weather prevents the men from going out to hunt and fish, the angakuk performs certain ceremonies and the weather may improve.

If there is a shortage of the fish, seals and whales on which the tribe survives, then the angakuk makes a journey to the depths of the ocean to visit the goddess who is responsible for the creatures of the sea.

An angakuk does not inherit his skills – a spirit possesses him, or sometimes her, without warning. Someone who wishes to become an angakuk may try to attract such a spirit by taking part in the appropriate ceremonies.

△ An angakuk who is going on a spirit journey will sometimes describe where he is going and what he sees to the rest of the tribe who are keeping his body company in the igloo.

ROPE TRICK

Indian magicians perform a magic trick which is so amazing that people are happy to pay for the privilege of watching it. The magician's tools are a basket containing a thick piece of rope, a large piece of white cloth, a knife and a flute – and he is always accompanied by a small boy.

When an audience has gathered, the magician starts to play a tune on the flute. The rope stirs in the basket and raises its head like a snake, swaying gently to the rhythm of the wavering melody. As the magician plays more vigorously the rope gradually extends to its full length until it stands straight up in the air. The lower end is a little distance from the ground and the upper end hidden by a cloud. Then the small boy climbs the rope and disappears into the cloud.

After a few moments the magician claps his hands and orders the boy to come down again. When he doesn't reappear, the magician climbs up after him, clasping the knife. To the horror of the audience there is a scream of pain and bits of the boy's body tumble to the ground.

The magician comes back down the rope and gathers up the bits in the white cloth. As he starts to play the haunting melody once more the bundle of cloth stirs and the boy emerges, safe and sound. The rope winds itself back into the basket, and the audience sighs with relief.

SHAMAN

A shaman is an intermediary between the human world and the world of the spirits. He inherits his magical powers at birth, but spends many years as an apprentice, so that he is an old man before he is able to practise his skills.

People ask for a shaman's help when there is a disaster such as famine or war. The shaman makes contact with the spirits by going into a trance. First he performs a series of rituals, which usually include drumming and singing, and when these have brought on the right conditions, he leaves his body behind to travel to the other world. There he meets up with the spirits of his ancestors, who tell him what must be done to relieve the suffering of his people.

If the shaman is asked to cure someone of a disease, then the spirits may accompany him to find the correct medicinal herbs for his patient.

◁ The most skilled shamans come from the freezing forests of Finland and Siberia. Not every child from a shaman family inherits the powers of magic. However, if a child is born with a full set of teeth and learns to speak much faster than is usual, the parents can be sure he will become a mighty shaman.

HUNTING MAGIC

Many hunters claim to have magical powers by which they can put a spell on their prey. Before setting out on the hunt, they draw a picture of the animal they are planning to chase. The picture shows the animal pierced by arrows and surrounded by hunters. To make the spell even more powerful, one of the hunters may pretend to be the animal and the others pretend to spear him.

Sometimes hunt dances are performed, and these are named after the chosen animals. Or hunting weapons may be smeared

▽ Hunting magic is probably the oldest known to humans. There are cave paintings of animals that are over 60,000 years old, showing the mammoths, bison and giant elk which the painters hoped to ensnare with their spells.

with the blood of mosquitoes, or any other stinging insect.

In addition, numerous rites and taboos are observed to make the hunt successful. These include rubbing the body with magic oil, painting it, bathing, and not eating certain foods.

NECROMANCY

Sometimes an evil wizard will try to foretell the future by communicating with, or even raising, the dead. In order to do this he has to shut himself away in a private place so that the spirit of the dead person will not be distracted by the presence of mortals.

First the magician fasts for several days, then he makes a fire

with herbs and rare ingredients. He must chant spells and the name of the chosen person tens of thousands of times before the spirit will reply. Raising the dead is so dangerous that only the totally desperate man will attempt it – the spells are far too perilous.

RAISING DEVILS

A really evil magician will sell his soul to the Devil. In return for Satan's favours, he makes a formal agreement pledging his body and soul to the Evil One, either at death or after a stated number of years. He signs the contract in his own blood, which symbolically conveys his life into the Devil's hands. The most famous magician who made this fatal bargain was Dr Faust.

VOODOO

Voodoo is a type of religious worship from the Caribbean that includes superstitious beliefs and practices, sorcery, serpent-worship and sacrificial rites. The word 'voodoo' comes from a West African word for a god or spirit, and the cult is still practised there.

During a voodoo ceremony, one or more of the worshippers goes into a trance and is possessed by a spirit. The spirits are known as loas, and like all spirits from around the world, their function is to help, comfort or torment human beings.

There are thousands of voodoo loas. They include not only gods of African origin, but also natural forces and objects such as the sun and the wind. The god Legba is always the first loa to be invoked in any ceremony. He is the spokesman and interpreter of the gods, and without his permission no other loa can enter into a worshipper. Legba is also the guardian loa of all gates and boundaries, so he is the god who protects homes.

The god of vegetation is Loco, who is often worshipped under the form of a tree. He gives knowledge of the secret properties of herbs, and consequently is also the god of healing.

The priests of voodoo are known as houngans. The sorcerers are called zobops. They possess similar powers to witches, wizards and sorcerers from other parts of the world, including raising the dead, flying through the air, appearing in a variety of different forms and supplying spells and magic potions. Houngans and zobops have to contact the loas in order to perform their magic.

Both houngans and zobops may be either male or female, but the males are more powerful. All of them have to do lengthy training before they are qualified to perform voodoo rites.

△ The Guede are a Voodoo family of death spirits, of which there are about thirty in number. They wear black top hats and frock coats, and look rather like undertakers.

There are thousands of books about fairies, goblins, magicians, witches and their doings. Go and look in your local library or your nearest bookshop and you will find an enormous choice of books to investigate.

The following list includes some classic stories that you should look out for and some books for adults which you might find interesting. You should be able to buy most of the children's stories in paperback.

The best collection of fairy stories can be found in the twelve **'Colour' Fairy Books** compiled by Andrew Lang. They are all available from Dover Classics in paperback and include the *Blue, Brown, Crimson, Green, Grey, Lilac, Olive, Orange, Pink, Red, Violet,* and *Yellow Fairy Books.*

A good collection of myths and legends from around the world can be found in the Oxford University Press' series: **Oxford Myths & Legends**.

Classic children's stories

Astercote, Penelope Lively (Mammoth). This author has written several other fantasy stories for children.

The Boggart, Susan Cooper (Puffin).

The Book of Three, Lloyd Alexander (Lion): there are another four books in this series if you like this one.

The Box of Delights, John Masefield (Mammoth).

Charmed Life, Diana Wynne Jones (Mammoth): there are another three books in this series.

Classic Fairy Tales, Helen Cresswell (editor) (Picture Lions). This author has written several other fantasy stories for children.

The Dark is Rising, Susan Cooper (Puffin): there are another four books in this series.

Five Children and It, E. Nesbitt (Puffin).

French Fairy Tales, Kara May (Dragon's World).

A Book of Goblins, Alan Garner (Puffin).

Grimbold's Other World, Nicolas Stuart Gray (Faber & Faber).

Hobberdy Dick, Katherine M. Briggs (Puffin).

The Hobbit, J.R.R. Tolkien (GraftonBooks).

The Irish Fairy Book, Alfred Perceval Graves (Dover)

King Solomon's Mines, Rider Haggard (Penguin).

The Magic World, E. Nesbitt (Puffin). This author has written several other fantasy stories for children.

Magic! The Story of Sorcery and Wizardry, Jim Hatfield (Horrible Histories, Watts).

The Midnight Folk, John Masefield (Mammoth).

The Moon of Gomrath, Alan Garner (Lion).

The Princess and the Goblin, George MacDonald (Puffin).

The Sword in the Stone, T.H. White (Puffin).

The Wizard of Earthsea, Ursula K. Le Guin (Puffin): there are another three books in this series.

The Weirdstone of Brisingamen, Alan Garner (Lion).

Adult books you might enjoy

Abbey Lubbers, Banshees & Boggarts – a Who's Who of Fairies, Katherine M. Briggs (Kestrel Books).

British Folktales & Legends, Katherine M. Briggs (Paladin).

Encyclopedia of Things That Never Were, Michael Page and Robert Ingpen (Dragon's World).

Encyclopedia of Myths & Legends, Stuart Gordon (Headline).

Fairies in Tradition and Literature, The, Katherine M. Briggs (Routledge).